Promoting Your Voice on School Safety

This hands-on guide helps teachers understand the complexity and humanity behind school safety and security issues—and their role in promoting, using their professional knowledge and expertise, a safe school environment.

While other books teach security techniques (lockdowns and drills), this unique resource focuses on acknowledging a teacher's role at the forefront of maintaining safe schools, as they spend the most time with students throughout the day. The book offers comfort and resources to these teachers on the front lines, with comprehensive guidance on how to identify, advocate for, and collaborate on school safety issues. It also provides invaluable information on classroom management, responding to trauma, striving for more equitable outcomes, and finding and using other voices.

Each chapter is filled with reflection questions, tools, and "What would you do?" scenarios, making this the perfect resource to work on with a colleague or study group. With the practical advice in this book, you'll feel more prepared and confident to tackle difficult decisions on both a small and larger scale.

Dr. Lori Brown spent 15 years in the schools of North and South Carolina as a teacher, administrator, and grant writer before transitioning to the world of proposal writing and professional learning for schools. Brown utilized her doctoral research to develop a formal definition of the construct of "violent writing" in K-12 schools.

Gretchen Oltman is an associate professor of interdisciplinary studies at Creighton University in Omaha, Nebraska. She has spent over two decades in education, from serving as a high school English teacher to leading in an administrative capacity at the university level. Much of her work revolves around violent student writing and the First Amendment.

Also Available from Routledge Eye On Education
(www.routledge.com/k-12)

17 Things Resilient Teachers Do
(and 4 Things They Hardly Ever Do)
Bryan Harris

Dear Teacher: 100 Days of Inspirational Quotes
and Anecdotes
Brad Johnson and Hal Bowman

Working with Students Who Have Anxiety:
Creative Connections and Practical Strategies
Beverly H. Johns, Donalyn Heise, and Adrienne D. Hunter

Everyday Self-Care for Educators: Tools and
Strategies for Well-Being
Carla Tantillo Philibert, Christopher Soto, and Lara Veon

First Aid for Teacher Burnout, 2nd Edition:
How You Can Find Peace and Success
Jenny Rankin

Promoting Your Voice on School Safety

A Practical Guide for Teachers

Lori Brown and Gretchen Oltman

Routledge
Taylor & Francis Group

NEW YORK AND LONDON

Cover image: © Getty Images

First published 2023
by Routledge
605 Third Avenue, New York, NY 10158

and by Routledge
4 Park Square, Milton Park, Abingdon, Oxon, OX14 4RN

Routledge is an imprint of the Taylor & Francis Group, an informa business

Library of Congress Cataloging-in-Publication Data
Names: Brown, Lori (Ph.D.), author. | Oltman, Gretchen A., author.
Title: Promoting your voice on school safety : a practical guide for
    teachers / Lori Brown and Gretchen Oltman.
Description: First Edition. | New York : Routledge, 2023. | Includes
    bibliographical references.
Identifiers: LCCN 2022020440 | ISBN 9781032363691 (Hardback) |
    ISBN 9781032281551 (Paperback) | ISBN 9781003331575 (eBook)
Subjects: LCSH: Schools—United States—Safety measures. |
    Schools—Security measures—United States. | School
    violence—United States—Prevention. | School
    management and organization—United States.
Classification: LCC LB2864.5 .B76 2023 | DDC
    371.7/820973—dc23/eng/20220727
LC record available at https://lccn.loc.gov/2022020440

ISBN: 978-1-032-36369-1 (hbk)
ISBN: 978-1-032-28155-1 (pbk)
ISBN: 978-1-003-33157-5 (ebk)

DOI: 10.4324/b23214

Typeset in Palatino
by Apex CoVantage, LLC

Contents

Meet the Authors

Dr. Lori Brown spent 15 years in the schools of North and South Carolina as a teacher, administrator, and grant writer before transitioning to the world of proposal writing and professional learning for schools. She has worked for large, global educator vendors designing literacy, leadership, and learning plans. Brown is licensed in K-12 second language instruction (German) and school leadership/administration. She utilized her doctoral research to develop a formal definition of the construct of "violent writing" in K-12 schools. She holds degrees from Davidson College, Furman University, and Western Carolina University and publishes in both the education and faith-based sectors. She makes her home, alongside her identical twin sister, in the mountains of western North Carolina.

Gretchen Oltman is an associate professor of interdisciplinary studies at Creighton University in Omaha, Nebraska. Oltman is a licensed attorney and holds a Ph.D. in educational administration. She has spent over two decades in education, from serving as a high school English teacher to leading in an administrative capacity at the university level. Much of her work regarding student and teacher safety revolves around violent student writing and the First Amendment in public schools. She is the author or coauthor of six books, including *What's Your Leadership Story: A School Leader's Guide to Aligning How You Lead with Who You Are*; *Law Meets Literature: A Novel Approach for the English Classroom*; and *Violence in Student Writing: A School Administrator's Guide*.

Introduction:
A Letter to the Reader

I want to make it clear that my actions on that day, in my mind, were the only acceptable actions I could have done given the circumstances," Seaman said Monday. "I deeply care for my students and their well-being. That is why I did what I did that day.

—Kusmer, 2018, para. 6

Dear Teacher:

In May 2018, when gunshots bombarded the halls of Noblesville West Middle School in Indiana, science teacher Jason Seaman did the only thing he could think to do—he ran toward the student shooter in an attempt to keep his students safe. His heroic attempt minimized harm to most students, although it came at the sacrifice of his own well-being, as the shooter shot him three times—once each in the abdomen, hip, and forearm (Rosenberg & Ortenzi, 2018). Seaman survived, along with a 13-year-old student who suffered even worse injuries. When asked about his decision to run toward rather than away from the shooter, Seaman explained that it was his care and compassion for his students that led him to run toward danger.

As experienced classroom teachers, we understand the passion and compassion that led Seaman to run toward rather than away, from danger, and we imagine you do, too. There's just something about teaching that makes all of us protective of our students.

DOI: 10.4324/b23214-1

We cannot help but feel a need to keep potential threats of harm away from students. But keeping students safe goes beyond the emotional need to show compassion. We live in a nation that, at times, hyperfocuses, criticizes, and micromanages school safety. As teachers, we are at the center of public discourse, and our livelihoods are threatened by political whims, underprepared school leaders, and a society that tells us to be quiet.

When we step into a classroom, we are obviously tasked with teaching content and skills, covering everything from English to earth science and from spelling to Spanish. As teachers, we teach. There is no doubt about that daily mandate. But teaching is so much more than textbooks and grading. In the process of teaching, we are engaging with other people—humans who are growing, thinking, and evolving right there in their school desks. We form relationships with our students—ones that cause us stress when they struggle and excitement when they excel. Our lives are intertwined as we walk alongside our students for however long they are in our classrooms—and sometimes many years after they leave. We want *our* students and *our* school to be safe.

But what exactly is a safe school? Is it different than a secure school? And how many times have you been asked to share your insights, opinions, or expertise about what conditions make your school or classroom safe or secure? In this book, we espouse that safety refers to the broader picture of both physical and social-emotional safety. Truly safe schools are ones in which students and teachers feel physically secure (secure schools = properly locking doors and windows, properly executed fire drills, closets devoid of dangerous chemicals, and more) and emotionally safe (they feel welcomed, valued, honored, appreciated, loved, invited, and listened to).

As educators, researchers, and authors, we explored the topic of safe classrooms academically through books, articles, and survey results and personally through one-on-one conversations with teachers, administrators, and support staff, largely because we believed that schools were making decisions about school safety without asking the teachers for their input. This, it seemed, was like putting a puzzle together but missing all four corner pieces. Why, in an attempt to create a safe school, would you ignore, silence, or talk over the people who work closest to the students day in and day out?

We firmly believe that the content you teach is of little relevance and impact if you and your students do no feel safe and secure in your classroom. Furthermore, we know that school and political leaders who ignore teachers as integral participants regarding school safety practices are neglectful. You should be invited and required to be active participants in how your school designs and implements all safe school practices.

Therefore, it is necessary to have a brutally honest discussion about the realities of school life across the country, particularly as conditions relate to your safety and to your school's willingness to allow you to advocate for equitable safe conditions for you and your students.

Why are teacher voices ignored or set aside in school safety discussions? We believe there are many reasons why teacher input is ignored, invalidated, or simply not welcome. These include everything from misinformed leadership, threats to job security, the influence of unions, the preconceived notions of biases and prejudices against student groups, and the influence of political or community activists.

We hope that your role as teacher never forces you into a situation like Seaman's. But life is unpredictable, and this unpredictability is also present in our classrooms.

Amidst changes and uncertainties, the one thing we want you to be certain of in matters of safe and secure schools is that your voice, opinion, and expertise can make an impact. Your safety and security matter as much as anyone else's, and your professional perspective of what students need makes you an invaluable voice in discussions of practices and policies. In short, we hope this book provides you with content and strategies you can employ to make your classroom and your teaching life safer.

—Your authors

1

Is My Classroom Dangerous?

I'm in my 25th year of teaching, and sometimes I just think about how much things have changed with the constant conversation about safe schools. Am I worried about an active shooter attack? No, not really, but neither were those other schools that were attacked in recent years. I don't like thinking about these things—things like drills, lockdowns, and guns in my school—but it's how we HAVE to think today.

—Sara, third grade teacher

Sara captures what many teachers feel today—an urgency to simultaneously work as a teacher and as a quasi-counselor and threat assessor who seeks to understand the complexities of mental health matters and safety concerns related to the students and stakeholders in and around her classroom.

You may relate to Sara and wonder what has become of education in today's schools. Guns, mass shootings, lockdown drills, natural disasters, pandemics, trauma-induced meltdowns, cafeteria fights, and significant depression among students are just some of the major topics that concern every educator—and rightly so. With non-stop news and social media coverage of the more intense tragedies, including social media accounts that announce which school found a gun in a student's backpack today, and the urgent and ongoing discussions about the value and impact of teachers, many of whom are leaving the profession because of these intense concerns, we just cannot escape the fact that we, as educators, do not always feel safe and secure.

DOI: 10.4324/b23214-2

Questions for the Reader

How does the constant media coverage of safe or unsafe schools impact your thoughts about this topic? What do you see in the news that reflects your own experiences?

One of the ripple effects of the global pandemic that emerged in 2020 is that educators began to speak about matters of safety and wellness on a more pronounced level because they couldn't stay quiet as they were forced overnight to start teaching from their sofas, and we honestly think their more pronounced voices were a positive pandemic outcome. Additionally, with many students needing to be educated at home by parents or family members, the role of the teacher (what do teachers do, say, and think on an everyday basis?) suddenly became widely exposed to those who had made prior assumptions, many of which were incorrect, about what goes on in today's classrooms.

With the advent of the pandemic, it was as if time stopped, and many parents and students began to see just how difficult (and rewarding) teaching can be. It was within this widespread shift in teaching and learning practices in a strange new world that the conversation turned to the value and importance of teachers and their vast knowledge about instruction, curriculum, assessment, managing student mental health, providing safe and welcoming classrooms, and much more. As families suddenly realized that "not just anybody" could teach algebra or struggled with the reality of trying to promote physical education with virtual lessons happening in local communities where everyone was locked inside, many suddenly recognized the true value of our teachers, and teachers realized that their voices had been silenced or ignored one too many times. This growing awareness led to a far more vocal teaching population, and this is something that we applaud and encourage. With the growing conversations about the role and needs of teachers arose an important element: suddenly our society seemed to understand that beyond teaching reading, writing, and math, teachers also have an extremely important role in keeping students safe.

Spend time in the classroom, walking the halls of your local school or even listening to news reports about current events in education, and you will recognize that today's schools are unlike those of prior generations. The influx of technology, the disparities of economic realities, the increase in student mental health issues, and the relatively high rate of teachers retiring or not returning to the classroom are just some of the challenges and opportunities that make today's schools a source of constant change.

Amidst this new national reality, one of the primary (and not new) needs of students is the need for stability (knowing who and what to expect on a daily basis) and safety: to be fed, cared for, acknowledged, and recognized. Keeping learners "safe" in every way possible, from protecting them from a global virus to making sure a tornado does not injure them or an intruder cannot get into the room, is a job that many teachers (and principals, directors, and superintendents) are not formally trained for at the university level, yet it is one of the educator's "key jobs" that directly influences a student's long-term success in the classroom.

Given this, we offer this resource to focus on the notion of what makes a "safe" school and what we, as teachers, need to know and practice to make our classrooms a safe place for every student, stakeholder, and for ourselves. Is it something we do? Something we say? Something we practice (e.g., a drill every month)? Is a safe environment even something we talk about in our grade level or content area meetings? When do we discuss it, and what is the result of that discussion? Are we too often making assumptions about safety that are not even true?

More important, we need to consider the decision-making processes related to safe and secure schools. Are those making decisions about safe school practices (e.g., leadership, politicians, directors, and more) able to hear and understand our concerns when it really matters? Do they seek our input on new safe school policies or ask us how we feel about having to implement rather unusual safe school practices? These are questions we need to ask if we're going to have an open, transparent dialogue about safe and secure schools.

But allow us to take a moment to ask—what do we REALLY mean when we say "safe and secure schools," and what do these terms have to do with academic teaching and strong leadership? Could it be that disruptions to what we do and expect to happen disturb everything from our peace and calm to our instructional strategy and student proficiency?

Consider the topics and concerns here that emerged from some practicing teachers and stakeholders. Each of these expressions and topics relates in some way to promoting fully safe and secure schools. Have you expressed or heard any of these concerns before or faced similar conditions or crises?

- One school had two fire drills, one hurricane drill, and one practice lockdown drill within the first two weeks of school.
- Within the first three weeks of school, one school pulled students out of class four times for assemblies and had a "picture day," which disrupted the start of school schedules significantly.
- One teacher suggested her principal start asking what he could remove from her plate before adding anything else because she and her colleagues were at a breaking point (this was less than one month into a new school year).
- One parent tweeted it was a good thing that teachers in her state were on strike (meaning schools were closed) because it meant her kid didn't have to face the real possibility of being shot at school.
- One teacher said that in one week, three of her colleagues fell ill to COVID, which left her asking if anybody really cared about the teachers.
- A safe school organization tweeted that violence outside of an Iowa school at dismissal time (involving six students with guns shooting randomly) left one student dead, two in critical condition, and only silence from the media because the shooting didn't involve a formal hit list.
- A teacher argued that although districts tell teachers to practice self-care, they then act floored and shocked when teachers tell them they are totally burned out and

need to make a career change (as if they didn't believe that teachers needed to care for themselves and give their bodies and minds rest).

◆ Teachers have posted in large waves across social media that they are simply burned out and want to quit.

◆ A local governmental official stated that the best solution for one local urban high school was to just burn it down.

Teachers are busy, tired, stressed, worn out, and overworked. So, too, are principals, directors, specialists, counselors, therapists, superintendents, and bus drivers. Schools are hard places to be today, meaning matters of safety and security can very much feel like an additional burden—something else we must add to an already busy day to satisfy school leaders and the community.

But promoting and maintaining safe classrooms are conditions that let us do what we do best: to teach. And, at the end of the day, these are conditions that allow us to avoid burnout and to teach with energy (as our minds are not distracted by the potential threats to safety). So, whether we like it or not and whether it feels like just one more thing, at some point we must participate in the decision making, conversations, and political chaos that surround the decisions and conditions that make a school safe.

Before we get any further, let us take a moment to define these terms so that we collectively understand why it is so critical for teachers to have a voice at the table in all matters of school safety and security.

Questions for the Reader

In your teacher preparation program, how much time did you spend learning about your role in promoting a safe school? What practices or processes have you learned during your experience in the classroom that ensure your classroom is safe? How do you know? And who knows about this?

Consider the question: What do schools need to be safe and secure? Some might argue a metal detector, fire drills, active shooter drills, chemical free cleaners, and more. But we believe we cannot fully respond to this question well until we break down the terms "safety" and "security," as they encompass so much more than what most people believe. Later in this chapter, we will dive into these terms with more depth, but first, consider the nuance between the terms.

If safety means we attend to mental and emotional well-being and wellness and security implies we attend to the physical state of things (this might include features like door locks, metal detectors, visitor check-in systems), then where should schools put the bulk of their money, and what categories of professional development should teachers demand? And how do we, as teachers, begin to share the magnitude of what really goes on in our classrooms in a way that community members and political leaders will understand, in order to make solid decisions regarding the future of our schools?

Former US President Bill Clinton all but answered this question more than 20 years ago following the 1999 Columbine High School mass school shooting. As he addressed a grief-stricken school and community, Clinton said: "We do know that we must do more to reach out to our children and teach them to express their anger and to resolve their conflicts *with words, not weapons*" (Clinton, 1999).

Think about that for a moment—words, not weapons. Clinton reminded us that the most proactive way that we can advocate for safer and more secure learning environments is to speak openly and loudly about the reality of our lived conditions, whether it is the trauma and ripple effects of poverty a student faces at home, the fear a student feels because of gang violence in the neighborhood, or the abuse a teenager faces at the hands of her partner. And speaking up and speaking out about our lived realities includes using our words, in honest and frank terms, to speak about our classroom lives and the reality of how traumatic they can be.

If our buildings are to remain functional places of learning rather than one of conflict, then lots of stories, including OUR stories, need to remain front and center because teachers are just one of many groups who regularly face and feel the intense physical, mental, social, emotional, and academic needs of today's students. Remaining silent about the challenges we face when tasked with safety and security plans, processes, and mandates that do not complement a place where students learn and teachers can thrive is no longer an option, and we know that many of you already know this. If you glance at social media, you'll find many teachers asserting something like, "We told you we were burned out years ago, and you didn't listen then, and you're not listening now as we walk out in groups. What does it take to make you hear and listen to us?"

In education, we often talk about the importance of student voice and how student input is valuable to the way a school functions—this is an important facet of this book, as we believe that the student voice must accompany the teacher's voice in safe school discussions. But do not forget the utmost importance of your voice—the experiences, opinions, input, and expertise you have as a classroom teacher who sees many students every day and every year. Your words mean something because you are the one who leads a classroom every single day, meaning you are the front line of protecting your students and responding to anything that might impact the well-being of those in your care.

It is sobering and difficult to think about writing extensive standards-aligned lesson plans when we are simultaneously asked to think about cyber threats, mass shooters, assaults, deadly diseases, incidents of bullying, and sexual assaults present in our schools. Unfortunately, many politicians, school leaders, and community members believe that teachers have superpowers and can teach perfectly, grade papers quickly, and rapidly secure window and door locks while tackling the gun-toting intruder, all while maintaining an aura of confidence rather than fear. But we are not superheroes. We are humans— very tired humans—attempting to work with the speed and intensity of a superhero who mitigates every global disaster before it hits, while keeping our attire, hair, and attitude in perfect form.

The reality is that we worry about many different things inside and outside of our classrooms, we are tired, and we often feel unheard, particularly when we are told to practice self-care but then given a stern lecture about how we cannot take personal days or miss school, even if we are sick, because there are not enough substitute teachers. We are teachers with hearts and emotions. We teach. We care. We give so much of ourselves in our classrooms, and our voices must be a key part of the national and broader global conversation about safe classrooms and schools. Keep this friendly mandate from your authors in mind as you join in the narrative presented across these chapters to consider all things specific to safe and secure schools.

From Bullets to Broken Windows: Maintaining Secure Schools

On February 14, 2018, a former student entered the doors of Marjory Stoneman Douglas High School in Parkland, Florida, killing 17 people and injuring 17 others. The aftermath of this tragedy included a cry that led to a Florida state commission recommending arming teachers in classrooms (Chuck, Johnson, & Siemaszko, 2018).

A year later, this recommendation became reality when the proposed legislation was passed, allowing public school teachers the right to carry firearms on school property (Dwyer, 2019). As one might imagine, this new law resulted in mixed emotions among Florida educators and the local community. Most importantly, it prompted the questions: Are guns in the hands of classroom teachers the best way to keep schools and students safe and secure? Are we now at a point in time where the only measure a teacher has to keep a classroom safe is by carrying a weapon?

The idea that a teacher's tote bag would contain his/her lunch, some graded papers, markers, highlighters, books, parent letters, and some bullets was sobering, if not even ridiculous. But we would argue that it was also energizing because it forced many to stop and ask if there is not a better way to keep kids safe at school. We would argue there is.

Questions for the Reader

How do you feel about teachers with guns in school, and why do you feel that way? Take a few moments to talk to fellow teachers about how they feel about this issue. Do you feel the same? Do you carry the same concerns? What can you identify as the most prevalent emotions represented in their comments?

School Security Defined

Security, as a general concept, refers to keeping people away from violence or danger. It is keeping the bad guys out and the good guys safe. Security often relates to how we approach our physical buildings or local environments, including the extent to which evacuation routes, door locks, metal detectors, background check procedures, the storage of dangerous chemicals or solutions, and visitor check-in processes are intact, logical, and helpful. When you post an evacuation route for fire drills, switch door locks so that they all lock from the inside, or use a phone that can dial the school's main office or 911, then you are experiencing real-world examples of school security tactics.

In broad terms, the phrase "school security" refers to everything from tornado and fire drills to preparations for regular electrical inspections and the selection and placement of school resource officers. School security is the part of schooling that helps us consider how we prevent and who helps us prevent the worst-case acts of danger or violence—from dangerous bullying behaviors, slippery floor accidents, cafeteria food fights, and the rare possibility of a mass shooting.

Examples of school security concerns include:

◆ Ensuring all doors to a building lock securely from the inside so outsiders cannot enter a building without authorization

- Utilizing internal security gates to keep access to classrooms blocked off as needed
- Practicing drills that include explicit evacuation routes, including fire drills, tornado drills, and active shooter drills
- Installing and monitoring school security cameras
- Ensuring any dangerous cleaning chemicals are away from student reach
- Installing effective "visitor sign-in" procedures that can screen whether someone is a harm to students
- Understanding how to respond to non-human threats (e.g., animals on campus)
- Badging protocols for all school staff
- Installing metal detectors (if relevant)
- Identifying rigorous "sign out" procedures so students cannot leave campus whenever they feel like it
- Designing and preparing school manuals that address these security protocols
- Completing school security audits

As you can see, many of these processes or practices involve clear boundaries specific to who is permitted in and who is kept out of a school building. Some utilize processes that require human intervention in rare circumstances, while others depend on a machine, weapon, or alarm doing the work. In fact, it has been said that following the tragic mass shooting at Marjory Stoneman Douglas High School in Parkland, Florida, state legislatures allocated more than $1 billion toward school security measures, with many offering grants to schools for improved security measures (Jordan, 2020). Yet current reports, as this book goes to print, show that school shootings, as of December 2021, were the highest they've ever been in our nation's public schools since 1970 (Statista Research Department, 2022). Reality check—none of these school security measures have made schools 100% safe.

Understanding a School Security Audit

Colorado, a state that for more than 20 years has significantly led the way to safer schools, a step taken in reaction to the aftermath of the tragic 1999 mass showing at Columbine High School, maintains a school safety audit protocol that addresses building features and practices that extend beyond drills (Colorado Department of Education, n.d.). Many tasks on the state audit deal with school security. Consider the following that each school in the state must address:

- ◆ School grounds are fenced. If yes, approximate height.
- ◆ Shrubs and foliage are trimmed to allow for good line of sight. (3'-0"/8'-0" rule).
- ◆ Bus loading and drop-off zones are clearly defined.
- ◆ There is a schedule for maintenance of . . . windows.
- ◆ Driver education vehicles are secure.
- ◆ Signage directing visitors to the main office are clearly posted.

The Colorado school security audit is comprehensive and serves as a great model for other states, but we can't help but ask the question: "Who is responsible for making sure these tasks are accomplished?" (and we don't mean strictly in the state of Colorado). Generally speaking, are our nation's districts on top of enforcing and reacting to such audits? Who is assigned the task of checking off each item on an audit? Is it the principal? The teacher? The school resource officer? The superintendent? The school secretary? The custodian? And then, who reviews these audits and follows through with making sure gaps are addressed? And with that responsibility comes accountability, so if we are asking teachers or other key school personnel to be at the forefront of checking off that they have firmly secured their classrooms, what tools or training are we providing them to do so?

Are Security Measures Enough to Keep Everyone Safe?

Despite our best intentions to keep schools safe and secure, security protocols (activities like active shooter drills) can unfortunately traumatize rather than alleviate student and teacher fears at school, as those who engage in regular mock drills may come to believe that their school building truly is unsafe on a weekly or monthly basis. Consider this: in recent years, a handful of schools conducted lockdown drills with weapons that were either shooting fake bullets (that felt like real bullets), involved execution style "mock shootings" of teachers, or even piped in sounds of guns hitting targets to make a drill feel more realistic.

Yes, you read that right. Piped in real bullet sounds for a more realistic (and fearful?) environment for the drills. In fact, one Indiana school chose to use fake bullets that left a few teachers with physical welts on their bodies and traumatized from the pain of being hit or from hearing the real screams of their colleagues who were hit with these fake bullets (Dickinson, 2019). Again, we ask, where are the teachers in this decision-making process?

Questions for the Reader

Put yourself in those teachers' shoes. What would you have done if exposed to this intense of a "drill," a drill that left you with bodily bruises and sleepless nights? Would you have spoken up? Would you have questioned anyone in authority? Do you see value in this type of drill? Discuss your answers with a teacher colleague and discuss how you would have raised your support or objections to these types of practice drills.

Additionally, schools with heavy metal detectors, security gates, fewer classroom windows, and other heavy security features can cause students to feel unwelcome at school. Instead of natural light, students and teachers may find themselves studying under fluorescent bulbs and ushered through intense security gates each day to begin the journey to their classrooms. We wonder if the perception of safety is destroyed simply by the atmosphere presented by walking through the front doors of a school.

All the metal detectors, locked windows, closed blinds, and monthly fire drills under the sun cannot and will not make our schools fully safe and secure environments, as locks and lights have little to nothing to do with the mental health side of schooling. A locked window does not address the terror a student feels in her/his head. A metal detector cannot detect the anxiety a student feels about an intruder entering her/his building after watching a school shooting segment on the evening news, nor can an evacuation route address the edginess a student feels from the student who secretly flashes a knife in the hallway.

The reason why security measures or protocols do not ensure fully safe schools is because security protocols cannot address safe school triggers. Safe schools are schools where there is attention to the mental health and social-emotional wellness of all stakeholders; where relationships are prioritized; and where verbal and social-emotional engagement between students, stakeholders, and staff matter. Having safe schools means we turn our focus from "what do we do if this happens?" to "how do we feel in this environment, and how can we promote a stronger sense of safety in every regard possible (physically, emotionally, and more)?" Let's take a moment to define exactly what we mean by the construct of safe schools.

Defining "School Safety"—Words, Not Weapons

When President Bill Clinton encouraged the grieving community of Littleton, Colorado, to embrace words over weapons, he recognized that a significant part of keeping schools secure is that of caring for students and teachers.

Safe schools consider the mental and social-emotional health as a priority, embracing a Whole Child Approach (2022). The Whole Child Approach helps us think about supporting all aspects of a student's development, including keeping them safe, promoting their emotional growth, and creating an environment rich in strong relationships and positive interactions. Students and their families need more comprehensive support today than ever before, yet they are often left out of the school safety planning process. And in many cases, parents are so concerned with fighting homelessness providing medical care, and meeting the basic needs of their students that they do not have the time to engage in discussions around safe and secure schools.

Today's students are not struggling solely with math and reading. Their basic needs are often not met, and rising inflation within two years of the global pandemic sent many into a downward spiral of despair. Families are in crisis, which leaves students in crisis and unable to learn or focus. Additionally, students who are living in challenging circumstances, where violence or emotional abuse might be present, may enter the school with altered expectations of appropriate behaviors, leading to more disruptive classroom conduct and difficulty in developing meaningful relationships with those at school.

What Makes a School Safe?

If drills and evacuation directives make our schools somewhat secure, then what makes us safe? Do we just need to feel happy to be a safe school? The following markers or characteristics of school life promote feelings of safety among students and teachers:

♦ Purposeful, engaging relationships between teachers and students that are consistent and predictable
♦ Mental health supports that available to support students in crisis
♦ A marked focus on improved social-emotional wellness and resiliency among students as an ongoing focus
♦ A trust between teachers and students
♦ A trust between parents and families and teachers
♦ Acts of aggression among students (e.g., bullying behaviors) are taken seriously and addressed through a mental health lens

- ◆ Teachers, teacher assistants, and other key staff feel comfortable conversing openly with school or district leadership about ongoing concerns
- ◆ Distributed leadership and decision-making protocols are a key part of the decision-making processes
- ◆ Embracing and valuing diversity among students, and tirelessly working to offer equitable learning and social-emotional supports and opportunities for all
- ◆ Ensuring diversity among voices and opinions of students and teachers is embraced, valued, and prioritized

In short, safe schools encourage student voices to move outside the confines of locked doors and active shooter drills to express emotion, insight, and acceptance. Safe schools use words, not weapons, to make everyone feel welcome and continuously work to create a school climate and culture that says, "We value you. We want you here. You are safe with us because you matter." Truly safe schools understand that if a student is upset because of a family crisis, he/she may not be able or willing to engage in learning on any given day, and it is not an act of defiance if they are not capable of engaging. Instead, the student is offered support in a meaningful and compassionate way.

How do we measure safe schools? With security, we explained that some schools embrace and utilize school security audits to check that the building is secure, but how do you really measure the extent to which students believe they can trust their teachers or that their peers value their work? Quite frankly, it is difficult, if not impossible. Yes, there are surveys, including bullying surveys, that focus on self-reported social-emotional beliefs or that measure efficacy, and researchers often hold purposeful conversations with teachers and principals who are observing classrooms daily, but truly understanding the mental health status of our people, starting with teachers and moving out to students, leaders, and others, is challenging. If we go back to the social responses in which teachers were all but screaming that they were burned out before COVID, and now they are on the brink of having a total breakdown, politicians or community members appear, at times, not to care. It then becomes immediately obvious that so much of the "safety" side of schooling is something we simply do not understand. We can survey people and hold focus groups, but sadly, it does not provide the full picture needed to take action because it can feel like we just talk, people and politicians listen, and then they forget what we said. There must be action with our voices for full comprehension, and that is what this book is designed to help us explore—how do we find a place for our voice to have meaning in matters of safe and secure schools?

Security vs. Safety: The Differences and Similarities

To review, a school might have flawless security measures (locked doors, armed guards, and constant surveillance), while its overall approach to safety (including that of students and teachers) is critically flawed. That is, regardless of the measures used to secure the school building, the same measures do not promote the feeling of well-being, protection, and trust that is built through human relationships, strong teacher efficacy, present and listening leaders, and a culture in which acceptance and respect is prioritized.

Prioritizing and Preventing Barriers to Security and Safety

School security vs. school safety—which deserves more attention? How do we balance the necessity for both? Should your school year start with writing an improved policy manual around drills, evacuations, and concealed weapons, or should it initiate a schoolwide emphasis on building leadership and resiliency skills that strengthens the heart, mind, and soul? Our answer: Do both. And we will repeat this response throughout the book—don't ignore either safety or security. Focus on both with your voice and actions.

There are many barriers to safe and secure schools, including:

- Lack of knowledge about policies
- Lack of communication about adopted practices and policies
- Missing professional development focused on recommended practices
- Inconsistent support for the implementation of safe and secure practices and policies
- Contradictory policies
- Reduced funding
- Sparse available meeting time
- Teacher or principal burnout and turnover
- High mobility rates among students

Each of these potential barriers is reason for concern, but we think our most critical barrier focuses on the lack of communication and professional development with and for teachers around safe *and* secure practices. Because schools have more teachers than counselors or administrators, it is fair to argue that teachers represent the largest group of stakeholders carrying the greatest burden for implementing and helping students understand key drills or practices for secure schools, as well as for securing their support of mental health and/or social-emotional capacity–building activities. Teachers do not get to pick one over the other—instead, we are expected to carry out both safe and secure practices while also carrying out our curricular responsibilities.

Although school districts must prioritize who leads in matters of school safety and security (who determines lockdown procedures or active shooter drill requirements vs. who identifies which social-emotional competencies and/or caring practices get implemented across the schools), at the end of the day, a district or individual school must determine that both are priorities, and they function in a symbiotic relationship with one another. To do this well, it must involve experienced teachers.

Is your local school safe? Is your local school secure? And do you know how you influence improvements in either or both categories? This book is designed to help you understand the critical role that you, the teacher, play, with helping to ensure both safe and secure schools exist for the good of everyone in your classroom (including yourself).

We encourage you to see your role in matters of school safety and security as (1) vital, (2) important, (3) insightful, and (4) necessary. As we work through this book, we will share practical strategies on how to articulate what is happening in your classroom with your students, how to put into words some of the darkest concerns you might carry, how to make your voice heard in a way that promotes safe engagement for you and your colleagues and stakeholders, and how to present yourself in a way that causes school leaders and community members to sit up and finally listen to what you have to say. And with that said, Chapter 2 explores the importance of our voices being heard on a much more public scale.

Reflective Questions for Teachers and Leaders

1. What preconceptions do you have about school safety or security in your building? Are there areas that concern you or cause worry?
2. What experiences do you have with security or safety issues in a school setting (i.e., your own education, your pre-service experience, or your exposure in teacher training?)
3. On a scale of 1 to 10, with 10 being extremely safe and 1 being not safe at all, how safe do you feel in your building?
4. What types of things do students talk about or share with you that deal with the safety or security of the school? What do you say when they share these things?
5. What do you wish parents and other community members understood about the challenges of keeping your classroom both safe and secure?

2

Finding and Using Our Voices

What is always missing at every level in education is the voice of the teacher. We are told what to do, but we are not asked what are the challenges in getting it done (Rizvi, 2019, para. 4).

—Nadia Lopez, principal, Mott Hall Bridges
Academy, Brooklyn, New York

Nadia Lopez, a former middle school principal in one of Brooklyn, New York's poorest areas, became famous when a former student featured on the *Humans of New York* blog identified Ms. Lopez as the greatest influence on his life. Interest in Ms. Lopez and in her school went viral, which led to her story being told on a broader scale.

Before stepping into the principal role, Ms. Lopez was a classroom teacher who did not feel heard. She worked with a student battling a mental health issue, coupled with a dangerous home life, that led him to engage in self-cutting. Upon expressing concern about the young man, little was done. He was only later hospitalized after writing a manifesto. Perhaps like many of you, Lopez wondered why no one was truly listening to her concerns about a student in apparent crisis and why it took the writing of a manifesto to engage a broader response.

This story begs the additional question: "When do we do something for a student in crisis?" Or "When do we do something for a teacher in crisis?" In Lopez's case, as is often the case in these situations, the student finally received some help, but nothing was offered to the teacher confronted with a self-mutilating student in crisis. We can only imagine how troubled

DOI: 10.4324/b23214-3

she felt about her student as his crisis likely deepened. Lopez was left to navigate her own emotions and reactions around this student crisis in isolation. How many of you reading this chapter have previously felt alone, struggling to know how to feel, respond, or express anger about a growing student crisis that does not appear to spark the level of reaction needed for a true change? If you have been there, you know it is not a pretty place to be, physically, mentally, or emotionally. And it is beyond demoralizing for a teacher trying to serve students well.

In Chapter 1, we introduced the idea that safe and secure schools require attention to unique challenges and that truly safe and secure schools only result when our teacher voices are at the decision-making table. And we want our voices at the table to be more than a token response to appease somebody, but instead, to represent a real opportunity for others to hear us and respond to our needs too. In this chapter, we dive into the dangers of not having our voices at the table and explore how we can assume a new title of teacher advocate. So, how can silence can be dangerous and even deadly?

Questions for the Reader

Have you ever been in Ms. Lopez's situation, knowing you have a student with significant challenges and feeling helpless because she/he is not receiving proper interventions or supports? If so, how did you advocate for your student? What could have been done differently? Who did you turn to for help?

While speaking up and speaking out may be intimidating as teachers, survey data reveal that we are actively seeking ways to be heard. The *Educators for Excellence* (2018) survey considered teacher voice across six areas of school life, including matters of school safety and discipline. Among the 1,000 preK-12 teachers surveyed, the following concerns emerged:

◆ Approximately one of three teachers feared for their physical safety sometimes or often at school.

- ◆ Of all the possible categories of violent acts (e.g., bullying, sexual violence, student assaults on teachers), the highest percentage of teachers (33%) identified gun violence or mass shootings as their top concern.
- ◆ When asked about the role of teacher unions, 70% of teachers reported that it was critically important for unions to ensure that schools remain safe and healthy work environments.

Stop and reflect on the finding that one of three, or 33%, of surveyed teachers, periodically or quite often, fear for their physical safety at school. In what other profession, outside of law enforcement, healthcare, or military-related roles involving combat, do one-third of employees fear for their physical well-being? Do sales managers, office assistants, physical therapists, or CEOs walk into their offices most days fearing their bodies may face assaults or acts of harm? While the global pandemic forced many offices to close, allowing staff to use home-based mobile offices, many people still report to physical buildings or locations (e.g., airports, bus terminals, restaurants) to get their jobs done. Do they, like teachers, walk in wondering who may assault them today?

While these survey insights prove helpful and tell us that teachers are far too worried about their own safety and security, surveys alone cannot capture the full phenomenon. Surveys capture one moment in time and are largely dependent on how a respondent feels that day or is experiencing life at that point in time, but again, surveys rarely dig deep enough to help us understand root cause analysis of growing fears, so that real action can be taken. For this reason, we argue that to begin to find value in our voices, we need to make sure we know how to gain a full perspective of what is happening.

The more we talk directly to teachers, the more we hear a common sentiment: Do teachers want to have safe and secure schools? Sure, just give us a voice. Just ask us what we think. We will tell you what can or cannot work. Why do our leaders and legislators not ask us more often what we think, experience, or feel?

Teachers honestly want to be heard because they know they have valuable information to share—they see the real world of chaotic classrooms, traumatized temper tantrums, student-on-student assaults, bullying, and so much more. They see it; they live it up close and personal; and they are expected to just go home, eat dinner, and come back the next day, acting as if nothing happened, with no one really stopping to ask them how they are doing or asking why a third of them fear for their personal safety. Even if they report on a safe schools survey that they witnessed three assaults, the questions rarely address how they responded, how they felt, or whether they felt prepared to respond to the crisis.

In the prior chapter, we spotlighted active shooter drills that used fake bullets, real gunshot sounds, and more, conditions that left teachers traumatized. Other situations in schools can similarly leave us traumatized or tortured, including the student who shows us the bruises they received from being slapped at home; the cafeteria fight that left one student's bleeding head pushed into the ground; or the student who accidentally ran through a glass pane and cut their leg to the muscles, requiring immediate emergency assistance.

The reality of teaching today is that we can and do face trauma and fear over many different things, including the trauma that accompanies working in a hostile work environment (yes, teachers bullying teachers is a real phenomenon) or the anxiety associated with parents or other stakeholders who take to social media to trash us and our reputations (more on this safe school concern in a later chapter). Trauma, fear, anger, and fatigue come in many different formats and stem from varied causes in the modern classroom; for this reason, we need to understand both the headline-grabbing and the non–headline-grabbing conditions that have caused many educators to walk away.

We believe that the global pandemic established a whole new level of trauma for today's teacher, the ripple effects of which are just now starting to come to light. Teaching changed, thanks to COVID-19, and our beliefs about safety and security changed, too. When the pandemic hit our nation's communities, the ever-growing list of traumatizing and terrorizing triggers for teachers suddenly added a new category that felt much deeper and more serious than most other concerns. It was a concern focused on teacher physical well-being—namely, serious questions about life and death.

One New York City teacher interviewed by *The New York Times* put it this way:

> Every day when I walk into work as a public-school teacher, I am prepared to take a bullet to save a child. In the age of school shootings, that's what the job requires. But asking me to return to the classroom amid a pandemic and expose myself and my family to Covid-19 is like asking me to take that bullet home to my own family. I won't do it, and you shouldn't want me to.
>
> (Martinson, 2020, para. 1)

The idea that the illness acted like a bullet that could destroy both this teacher and her immediate loved ones is simultaneously sobering and almost unbelievable. Schools and educators have long voiced concerns about the potential for mass shootings or other weapons-related acts that could result in the loss of life or harm to physical bodies, but this threat was new, and it carried with it a new response from teachers. The novelty of this response focused on the idea that to date, teachers had largely done what they were asked to do, even if it meant staying in violent-laden schools, teaching students who had previously assaulted other teachers, and more, but with this new threat to teachers and their families, they used their voices to say: "We aren't moving."

Teachers would stay home and risk insubordination or being fired before they would threaten their families with an illness they feared. We like to say that this response represented Teacher Voice 2.0, if we think about the prior teacher voices that were occasionally listened to as Teacher Voice 1.0. Finally, somebody was seriously listening to teachers, and it wasn't just the superintendent, the local community, or an elected official. This time, it was the whole world hearing us loudly and clearly on the television and on social media as people had nothing but time to listen.

This real teacher concern and resulting professional defiance in the face of potential danger brought to light the reality that teachers' voices had been silenced too often, while also bringing forth another set of new questions about whose voices carry the most weight in these sobering stand-offs. If other voices matter more than teachers' voices, then what does this imply to teachers and their families about communities that may argue they want equitable, diverse voices at the table?

What if, in an attempt, to make our voices heard about the trauma or fear we feel about active shooter drills, tornado drills, or teaching amidst community illness or outbreak, we learn that only select voices will be heard and considered or that we will be forced to continue doing our jobs even when we feel that we are in a direct line of threat? For many teachers living and working through the COVID-19 pandemic, new realities came to light. When many realized that their voices might not be the voice of priority, they left the profession. Enough was enough, and they were tired of being silenced and ignored.

For others, the pandemic caused them to suddenly begin to speak up and speak out after years of staying far too quiet. It awakened something in teachers to have their say, and we need for these voices to be loudly awakened in conversations about your safety and security at school. Sadly, when we stay quiet, there are often unintended ripple effects that impact the wellness and safety of others.

Consider our special education teacher friends Sara and Frida and their experience of realizing that their voices had to be heard on a greater scale if their students with physical and mental disabilities were to be kept as safe as everyone else.

Valuing the Voice of Experience

Sara, an elementary teacher, and Frida, a retired special education teacher, experienced firsthand what happens when nobody asks the teacher how safe school matters should be handled.

Sara has been teaching at the elementary level for nearly 25 years—a true veteran in the field. But despite her role on many school committees; a strong professional relationship with a principal who often asks for her curricular and instructional opinions; and a clear teacher leadership role that provides the opportunity to mentor newer, younger teachers, Sara described to us a safe school activity that left her shaken.

At the beginning of her 22nd year of teaching, Sara returned to school in August, prepared for the first month's fire drills. Sara's school, like all public schools, conducts a fire drill every month to meet state mandates for school safety and security. For years, Sara and her students exited the building upon hearing a mock alarm by rounding the corner outside of her classroom, moving through exit doors and congregating in the bus parking lot, but this particular year, without warning, she and colleagues were notified of a change in the evacuation route and assembly spot, which puzzled Sara.

This year, Sara's class would be required to exit the building by walking down a long hill and congregating in an empty field. But there was just one problem with the empty field—it ran along a major roadway with heavy traffic and speeding cars. Without a fence, it was easy for elementary-aged students to get dangerously close to vehicles traveling at highway speeds, a condition that caused great distress among the teachers.

Additionally, the new evacuation site presented another challenge: If this was to be the permanent evacuation site for other drills, including active shooter drills, then students would be left more vulnerable than before, as the field provided no space to hide or flee outside of the busy road. An active shooter with a functioning weapon could have taken out the entire class as they stood in the field with nothing to shield their bodies. Finally, the new, longer evacuation route with a lengthy hallway would pose a distinct problem for Sara's students with mobility challenges, meaning a swift exit was simply not possible. She had one student who used a wheelchair.

Questions for the Reader

Have you ever been in Sara's shoes, feeling as if the decisions made above your head put you or your students at greater risk of harm? If so, how did you respond? Who did you turn to for help?

High school teacher Frida faced a similar unsettling school evacuation process. As a special education teacher working in a specialized "school within a school" for students with severe cognitive and physical disabilities, Frida knew a school evacuation drill was no easy task and always meant that she and her fellow colleagues spent the rest of the day helping agitated students calm down after the disruption.

In fact, she dreaded each month's regularly scheduled fire drill because the screeching alarm agitated some students and sent others running for cover. With many of Frida's students using wheelchairs or facing extreme sensitivity to loud noises like fire alarms, the monthly fire drill often resulted in meltdowns and slow evacuation processes. But the evacuation became even slower one November morning when the elevator broke and there was no way to evacuate those in wheelchairs. The only option was to walk the entire length of the building (a good quarter of a mile walk) to exit via a very long wheelchair-accessible ramp.

As the weary teachers and students approached the ramp to finally exit a potentially burning building, they heard loud voices and madly waving arms saying, "Stop; you can't exit here. You can't exit here. This isn't your evacuation spot," to which the teachers, with wheelchairs in front and behind them, looked at one another thinking, "How are we to evacuate our usual way on the second floor with no working elevator? Do they really expect us to turn around and reverse our steps when we can see the door ahead and we've already pushed our physically vulnerable students across the entire campus to find an exit?" At this moment, Frida and her team felt deep frustration and anxiety, and their growing anger led them to boldly push the doors open and march outside via the route they were told they could not take. Again, no one had asked for their input or the unintended consequences of poorly thought-out changes.

What Would You Do?

Put yourself in Frida's situation. What do you do at this moment, considering that speaking up will likely put you at odds with your administration? Write your response in the space provided here:

Perhaps you are wondering why we shared Sara and Frida's stories. Did we do this to paint school leaders or school safety experts in a bad light? Absolutely not.

We firmly believe that administrators, directors, and safety experts want to keep everyone safe and often give great attention to drill details, working with local law enforcement and safety experts to make sure their evacuation plans, crisis responses, and more are in alignment with recommended and research-based best practices. Attention to detail is critical by these experts, and we must allow room for them to do their jobs without interference.

But too often we have heard from various special education teachers that the unique evacuation needs of those with physical or mental health challenges are forgotten in the larger picture of safe and secure schools. And for Sara and Frida, their evacuation experiences left them feeling greater fear and worry—not less. A properly handled drill or safety exercise should not cause more distress to any student or teacher. It may spotlight things we have not thought about (e.g., How do students in wheelchairs exit a building well, especially when elevators malfunction? How do students with autism who are triggered by loud noises handle fire drills?), but are teachers actively being sought out for their own knowledge of the school hallways, traffic patterns, and potential danger spots?

The evacuation challenges faced by Sara and Frida could have been avoided had their voices been welcomed in the identification of evacuation routes and procedures. This is why this chapter is about making your voice heard. When our voices are not heard, either because we are too afraid to speak up or because we get the message that our voices are not wanted, we face a crisis, a crisis of distrust, frustration, and silence none of which will ever lead to improved job satisfaction.

Consider the significance of having your voice silenced and whether it is often intentional or unintentional.

The Pain of Not Being Heard

Connecticut teachers know a thing or two about choosing to speak up when it appears no one is listening to their concerns.

Sample headlines related to Connecticut schools have included

◆ "Mold, Rodent Droppings, Extreme Temperatures: Connecticut's Schools Are Falling Apart and Making Students and Teachers Sick" (Andrews, 2019)
◆ "Troubled Schools on Trial: When Poverty Permeates the Classroom" (Thomas, 2016)
◆ "Almost a Dozen Hartford Schools Could Contain Dangerous PCBs" (Gutierrez, 2019)

Before the mold, mildew, and rapidly increasing results associated with the trauma of poverty, though, was a growing concern about student behavior and the physical and mental health threat it posed to staff. In 2018, teachers shared real-world episodes of teacher victimization at the hands of students, begging legislators to pass a bill to address classroom safety and disruptive student behavior.

The testimonies of burned out, injured teachers were nothing less than heartbreaking. Consider these direct teacher quotes (Connecticut Education Association, 2018, para. 5):

- ◆ "A good friend and colleague of mine had to give up her running hobby after a student kicked her so hard that her leg fractured and never fully recovered."
- ◆ "I have been violently shoved around in my classroom. The administration and resource officer did nothing. They blamed me."
- ◆ "I know of several students who have assaulted a teacher either with threats or with physical violence, and the interventions taken in all cases were not enough to ensure the safety of our staff and students."
- ◆ "My colleagues who have been assaulted have left the profession because they felt abused and not supported by the administration."
- ◆ "I have been hit, kicked, scratched, and pushed."

Think and Write

What is your immediate reaction to these teacher testimonies detailing physical assaults? What resonates with you? What shocks you? Write your thoughts in the space provided here:

Connecticut teachers are not alone. Scanning headlines from nearly every state will yield similar concerns shared by teachers in virtually any type of classroom. While we know these events can be sparse, we also admit that in some districts, these types of attacks on teachers are frequent and readily dismissed by school and community leaders.

For the teachers who are directly impacted—those who arrive at work worried about their own well-being—the issue is magnified in its relevance. Similar stories of teacher attacks, including physically aggressive students who pose a physical threat to teacher safety and security and stories of teachers working in horrific conditions can be found in nearly every state. Alarming headlines or self-written blog posts that have spotlighted how seriously these threats can be include:

◆ The Philadelphia teacher who worked in an asbestos-laden classroom for 30 years, only to acquire mesothelioma, an aggressive cancer often caused by asbestos (Ruderman & Graham, 2019)

◆ The Richmond, Virginia, teacher, Keri Treadway, who regularly set out mouse traps and cleared away mice droppings before students entered the classroom each morning (Truong, 2019)

◆ The former Indiana teacher who confessed in a blog post that she experienced the following from students: A student threw a literature book at her head; she was stabbed with a pencil, shoved, and kicked in the leg; she dealt with student outbursts that could not be controlled; she endured a student verbally calling her a "bitch" for 30 minutes; and she had two students who threatened to kill her (Barnes, 2019)

Such headlines make us wonder how teaching became a profession in which teachers have been expected or conditioned to remain quiet when the conditions under which they are expected to function well are deplorable, unsafe, unhealthy, and ultimately very dangerous to their long-term health. How many other professions expect employees to clear away mice droppings or work around cancer-inducing materials to get the job done, and why have we routinely ignored these concerns when teachers speak out about them? Do we just need to point fingers at our educational leaders and say it is all their fault? No, we will not.

Let us be clear. We do *not* believe that most school districts or local schools knowingly want to put any teacher or other school or district staff in harm's way. Anyone who has been an educational leader will tell you immediately that we sometimes do not know what we do not know. In other words, there is so much happening in our schools at any given moment that we cannot even begin to properly address all concerns simultaneously, and administrative red tape, procedural issues, or a simple lack of funds can make progress with growing concerns futile.

Even when superintendents, directors, and principals want to respond well, sometimes the funds, the verbal or emotional support, or the state legislative greenlight are not there to fix the problems. Most school districts do not have a few million dollars available to start building a new school when an entire wing is suddenly deemed hazardous, nor do schools regularly have an excess of unused funds to suddenly replace all locks, windows, and doors while paying teacher bonuses for extra duties that relate to school safety.

We acknowledge that school leaders face significant challenges in keeping teachers safe and secure. Although teachers may think that nobody really wants to listen to them, the reality may be that their voices are heard quite clearly, but districts and schools lack funds, community support, or the manpower to even begin to address unsafe conditions. It is unfair to assume that no action means leaders do not care because we have often discovered that they care very deeply.

But there must be balance, and we continue to hear that teachers are voicing their concerns while being met with silence and inactivity. So, what is the solution if it feels like we are talking to a wall, being met with a "Thanks for sharing. Now return to teaching" attitude?

We believe that part of the solution (not the entire solution) is to begin to turn your voice into a microphone of advocacy. We challenge those of you reading this book to start each school year with a newly appointed title: You are not *just* a teacher. Instead, you are now an empowered "teacher advocate." You are bold, confident, worthy, and heard. Your work is based on your professional expertise and field experiences, and this alone gives you the justification to be heard and acknowledged. This alone gives you the right to say, "I won't teach the student who tried to assault me."

Advocacy is really hard work, and speaking up when it feels unpopular or unwanted is not easy, especially when we fear that becoming a vocal advocate will cause us to lose our jobs. But we believe that one of the best safe and secure school actions each teacher can take is that of learning to be his or her own best advocate. If we do not boldly voice when and why we feel unsafe or insecure, then nobody else is going to care that we do. Let us consider some tips to advance our elevated title of teacher advocate.

Teachers as Advocates

Teachers' voices should be prioritized when it comes to the expertise needed to make sound school decisions. Brown and Buskey (2014) explain that teachers are the **closest** to what is happening in the classroom (on the front lines); know students the most intimately; and are best prepared to share knowledge around matters of school safety, curriculum, and instruction. Selecting the right math curriculum is just as critical as selecting a compassionate way to engage the school community in active shooter drills.

Consider some ways teachers, in more recent years, have started to blend their roles as instructional leaders with advocacy:

- ◆ More teachers are running for political offices (meaning that in many integral roles that make decisions about schools, people who have actually worked in schools are able to lend their expertise to the legislative process).
- ◆ Teachers across multiple states are engaging in frequent strikes to protest the lack of pay and supplies (meaning a greater impact is felt when students cannot attend school, there are not enough substitute teachers to hold classes, or entire districts are disrupted).
- ◆ Traditional public school teachers are speaking publicly about the way that charter schools harm their districts financially, as each student who moves to a charter school results in loss of per pupil funds for the school left behind (opening a larger conversation with lawmakers about the

proper use of public funds and how these funds should be dispersed for educational purposes).

◆ Social media has increasingly become a platform for teacher connections and conversations. National organizations such as the National Education Association and Kappa Delta Pi have even worked to explain to educators how to use social media for advocacy efforts, offering advice on messaging and framing ideas to reach a wider audience.

Catone and Saunders (2018) applaud the growth in teacher advocacy but simultaneously argue that too few fail to realize the critical nature of teacher voice at times:

> The list of places where teachers are raising our collective consciousness about woefully inadequate teaching and learning conditions and grossly underpaid salaries is growing steadily. West Virginia. Oklahoma. Kentucky. Arizona. Colorado. Puerto Rico. North Carolina. These recent teacher actions are forcing policymakers and education reformers to reckon with teacher power and voice in new ways. Though it should seem obvious that when making policy about education, lawmakers and reformers should be listening to the voices of those they most primarily affect—teachers and students—sadly, this is not the case.
>
> (para. 1)

Social media has created a wider network of collective voices. Teachers who find success challenging the destructive norms of school safety drills or practices can share their expertise with teachers in different states or in different countries. Rural teachers are no longer isolated from their urban counterparts, and their voices are now merging together to help the greater public understand the unique challenges they face. Teachers, it seems, have found a way to connect outside of the walls of their individual schools, in turn magnifying the potential impact when they choose to speak or act.

The Fear of Advocacy

We know that using our voices as teacher advocates at the principal's or superintendent's doorstep, or better yet, at the steps of the state capitol, can be frightening and intimidating. When North Carolina teachers chose, in 2019, to engage in strikes protesting their poor treatment by state legislators who had repeatedly destroyed state funding for classrooms, districts did not hesitate to imply that their advocacy efforts would put them in violation of local or state policy and could threaten their job security.

The state's response to the threat of teachers speaking up was a direct effort to silence their voices. This was what we might call an act of intimidation. But the irony of the intimidation, as highlighted by Parmenter (2018), was that the state's professional standards for teachers includes, in sections 1c and 1d, attention to **teachers as leaders** who:

- ◆ Strive to improve the profession
- ◆ Contribute to the establishment of good working conditions
- ◆ Participate in decision-making structures
- ◆ Promote professional growth

Fear of job loss or for being targeted as a "quasi enemy" of the state was enough to keep many teachers quiet, as is often the case. Teachers need their jobs to pay the mortgage, to put their children through college, and to care for their aging and elderly parents. They also need health insurance. They cannot easily shift from school to school or job to job. They have families that depend on their incomes and the benefits of their jobs and they are ingrained as citizens in their communities. Teachers should not become easy targets because they choose to speak about their job conditions or concerns. Furthermore, speaking out should not put a teacher's job in jeopardy.

Advocacy work can be daunting, so please hear us clearly when we say that we are not pushing you to lay down this book and immediately start calling your state senators to express anger over what happened last school year. You may choose to call your state-level legislators at some point, and we encourage you to be respectful and bold when you do so, but we firmly believe that there is also much you can do in your own school that invokes an informal advocacy role that can be just as effective. You can be a teacher leader in your classroom, in your hallway, and in your school cafeteria, just as well as you can be on the steps of the state capitol.

All of us can take a critical role as teacher leaders and advocates, and it is this idea that we want you to keep firmly embedded as you journey through the remaining chapters. Ask yourself: How can I, as a teacher leader in my building or district, find a place that improves and expands my school's capacity to effectively address all matters of safe and secure schools? As you reflect on this question, we have some ideas that may prove helpful.

Meaningful Ways to Amplify Your Teacher Voice

Consider these avenues for amplifying your teacher voice:

- ◆ Believe you deserve what you are advocating for—that is, you do not need to teach in poor conditions with minimal support just because the budget is tight or because you teach students with challenging needs. You deserve to be treated like any other professional with dignity, respect, and admiration.
- ◆ Utilize your expertise in teaching and learning; consider not only attending school board and district leadership meetings but also testifying at these events.
- ◆ Tailor your message for your audience. Whether you are writing a letter to the editor, addressing the school board at a public meeting, or speaking to the parent–teacher association (PTA), prepare your ideas to adequately reflect what the audience can tend to. It makes no sense to complain to the PTA about the school board or vice versa. Recognize and plan for the audience you want to hear you.

- ◆ Engage with social media in a responsible way that reflects professionalism.
- ◆ Participate in union activities rather than being a bystander. Run for elected office in the union. Meet with union leaders.
- ◆ Identify how specific school actions impact burnout, well-being, or workload in measurable ways.
- ◆ Know your rights and speak to those. Contractual responsibilities should not quell the necessity to improve working conditions.
- ◆ Be specific in what you need (avoid laundry lists of everything that is wrong) and provide creative solutions that may be outside of the box in traditional decision-making routines.
- ◆ Anticipate failure. Sometimes change takes a long time and our initial attempts to instigate new ideas can fail quickly. Accept this and move forward. Make changes where you can and continue to refine your message. Listen to your critics and adapt and adjust accordingly.

Teacher Leadership and Advocacy for Safe School Topics

As a teacher advocate, find a new place for yourself among school or district committees. See yourself in the broader light of mentor, advocate, coach, and consultant. Realize that you have a unique front-line perspective from which other district staff can benefit. Realize and promote that your experiences in the classroom matter and should be part of the conversation. And never forget that there are select safe and secure school topics that only a teacher can fully understand.

Consider these examples to share with your leadership team as you advocate for a stronger voice in the chaos and confusion of the best safe and secure school policies and procedures:

- ◆ **Drills and dangers:** Teachers should be called on to assess the efficiency of current evacuation and active shooter drills or to lead drills. Additionally, teachers should be allowed to be part of the drill debrief.

Teachers, compared with school administrators, may see that barriers, challenges, or unanticipated concerns are overlooked by higher level leadership. A prime example is the rapidly emerging information highlighting the added stress and anxiety that participation in active shooter drills is causing for students and staff (Blad & Will, 2019). For a leader who is most concerned with the efficiency of such a drill, she/he may fail to recognize the mental health concerns associated with practiced drills. Additionally, the teacher, may be able to identify ways that current class schedules or building practices hinder proper evacuation processes. Teachers who have ideally formed meaningful relationships with their students may have insights or understandings that no school safety planner could anticipate. Pair new teachers with more experienced teachers to promote a collaborative investigation.

♦ **Mental health and student wellness:** Because teachers understand, better than most, the extent of student mental health concerns, as they see anxiety-laden and struggling students on a regular basis and can help school-based mental health staff effectively identify trends of behaviors, including escalating aggressive behaviors, it is important to let teachers, in partnership with school counselors or psychologists, lead the charge for proper social-emotional and mental health supports. If teachers believe that students will benefit from positive community mentors, then let teachers lead efforts to establish such a program. If teachers recognize that test anxiety is causing a subset of students to shut down and become more aggressive, then allow teachers to recommend new ways of approaching the teaching and learning process, with less of an emphasis on testing outcomes. Supporting the overall wellness of our students should never be the single task of any given administrator or counselor.

♦ **Response to frightening voices:** The most significant red flag that a student is struggling with anger or frustration is often found in written or verbal expressions of a desire to harm someone. The words that students include in journals, creative writing activities, biographies, oral presentations, or in hallway communications with peers provide great insight to student instability or worsening social practices. In fact, many school shooters wrote of dark, dangerous, or violent themes in school-based assignments prior to committing their final deadly acts. Because the Virginia Tech shooter wrote of such violent and disturbing themes prior to committing the deadly 2007 mass shooting, Virginia Tech established a formal procedure for how to respond to disturbing or questionable student expressions. While it is wrong to ask a teacher alone to take a frightening student text/utterance and determine on the spot whether he/she is threatening, the teacher voice must be part of the broader conversation of a school or district threat assessment team looking at student expression and trying to determine how this triangulates with other inputs to form a picture of risk.

Questions for the Reader

Is teacher representation present on the various decision-making teams within your school and district? Do some research to understand how decision-making committees are formed and how membership is determined. If you see gaps, develop a list of creative roles that would promote teacher engagement around the topic of safe schools. Volunteer to take one of these key roles, supporting your school as an active participant with decisions around drills, mental and physical wellness, and school response to disturbing student communications. If you see committees that lack teacher input, identify ways to propose membership changes and to ensure teacher membership is written in policies and bylaws.

Prioritizing the "Professional" as a Teacher Advocate

It is one thing to be a bold advocate, but it is an entirely different thing to be an advocate who makes people run and hide because of the abrasiveness of your approach.

As you begin to see yourself as a teacher advocate pushing for more than just the right to teach but rather pushing for the right to teach in a fully safe and secure environment, it is critical to remain professional and to respect the dissonance that comes with dialogue around sensitive topics. Afterall, what if the very thing you are advocating for will actually do more harm than good? We must realize that we can learn from those with whom we disagree and we want to learn to listen to our opponents, too. To that end, consider these tips for effective advocacy:

- ◆ Be professional and rely on your classroom experiences to build your case. Rather than focusing on the emotions of your position (passion, enthusiasm) advocate for student-centered policies and decisions that protect the learning environment.
- ◆ Plan and build a consistent message. A thoughtful argument should include two or three talking points that can be quickly shared and described. Do not waver on the "what if's" or hypotheticals that are present in most arguments—keep your mindset based on facts and repeating a consistent, honest advocacy piece.
- ◆ Use reason, not emotion. Acknowledge that others will see things different from you or that their hands may be tied financially or politically in a way that prevents them from enacting change immediately. Listen to what your opposition is saying. Is it based in fact or opinion? Use facts and real-life experiences to invite an audience.
- ◆ Protect the integrity of your teacher voice. This means making sure you know the full picture of what you are talking about so you cannot be accused of being just another random ill-informed voice. What you advocate for should be true, based in evidence and should always improve teaching and learning conditions. Admit where

there are faults in your argument or where your school might be different from others. Do not pretend to speak for all teachers but speak your truth.

In this chapter, we advocated for your front-line expertise to play a role in forming your voice as a teacher advocate. There is simply too much on the line to stay silent when teachers, and other educational professionals, face physical or mental health dangers or feel unsupported. You can become a voice that elevates the profession well, and we urge you to take your new title and personalize it to your local and state needs as a way to be a voice for others, too, but we simultaneously urge you to advocate in a way that is professional, purposeful, and meaningful. Stay focused, stay informed so your concerns are well documented and factually accurate, and practice with your voice so you are comfortable in your new role. As a result, the safety and security of the entire school community will advance.

Take Action! Ways Teachers Can Activate Their Voices

1. Prepare your public persona. Attend and contribute to school board meetings. Speak up at staff meetings. Engage with school leadership one on one.
2. Attend staff developments, virtual summits, and web-based seminars that build your expertise in teaching and learning. The more you know factually about your profession, the more you can persuade others with facts.
3. Call your state and federal representatives to express your position regarding legislation and political positions.
4. Become a competent communicator, both in writing and speech. Document your concerns in writing. Share your concerns in writing, not just through hallway conversation. Keep copies of repeating issues so that you can draw on previous communications to refresh memory or back up claims of prior issues.

5. Represent your peers through responsible, ethical behavior on the job. Limit complaining and gossiping. Demonstrate your commitment to teaching through your everyday actions.
6. Testify in political hearings, legislative sessions, or any other public forum where teachers can be directly impacted.
7. Distinguish between being an advocate and an adversary—no one wants to listen to a teacher who is actively trying to dismantle education. Instead build your arguments on strengthening schools and teachers.
8. Partner with parents. Believe it or not, parents can be some of the best people to advocate for and with you. By building strong parent relationships, you will most likely find allies who can replicate your voice into the community.

Teacher Talk: Reflective Questions for Teachers and Leaders

1. Would you feel comfortable talking to a school administrator about safety or security concerns? Why or why not?
2. What thoughts enter your mind when you see/hear politicians and other non-educators speaking publicly about issues dealing with teaching, learning, and school safety?
3. Have you ever assumed the role of "teacher advocate?" If so, describe that experience.
4. Would you volunteer for a teacher leader role in matters of school safety for your local school? If not, why not?
5. What long-term consequences could occur if teachers' voices continue to be silenced or left out of school decision-making processes?

3

Building a Safe and Secure Classroom

One day as I was leading a lesson on quadratic equations, my assistant principal, Ms. Childs, walked into the room to observe my teaching. It was a hot day, and the air conditioning wasn't working, so we had the windows open. As luck would have it, as Ms. Childs walked in the door, a bee flew into the room and stung one of my students, Serena, on the arm, and all hell broke loose. Serena screamed when she got stung, jumped up quickly, and knocked her desk backwards toward Arjun, the student behind her. Arjun thought she did it on purpose, so he retaliated by pushing his desk and yelling at Serena, and everything went downhill from there. My classroom suddenly looked and sounded like a war zone and poor Ms. Childs just stood there shaking her head.

—Kimi, 10th grade algebra teacher

In the introductory chapters, we briefly defined the concept of safe and secure classrooms and encouraged you to find your voice and use it for good to advocate for improved conditions that keep everyone (including you) physically, emotionally, and socially safe and secure. But you may be wondering where to start with this new advocacy role. If you're going to speak up, then do you start by voicing concern about the unlocked doors on the back side of the gym, complain about the teacher who never completes the fire drill correctly, or argue that your school needs a metal detector to prevent weapons making it into the building?

We have and will continue, throughout this text, to encourage you to find your voice and take action, but we have yet to really explain what that means on a day-to-day basis. In Chapter 3, we

DOI: 10.4324/b23214-4

start by recommending close attention to the basics—rules, regulations processes, and procedures—otherwise known as the building blocks of orderly classrooms, and topics that you likely encountered in the first few months of your teacher preparation program.

Discipline or management is noted as one of a teacher's greatest challenges in the workplace. In fact, a survey of teachers in Oklahoma City found teachers painting a startling reality around classroom management or discipline (Willert, 2017). Teachers reported that they spent far too much time on significant disciplinary actions, and chronically misbehaving students.

Without doubt, one of the greatest distractions a teacher faces when these conditions become our lived reality (e.g., the teacher has to teach the student who just tried to assault her) is the loss of respect for the teacher's authority. How many of us have faced difficult student behaviors that shut down learning for a class of 30, only to realize that the student faced no significant disciplinary action and was back in the classroom the next day?

When we consider the distinction between classroom discipline and management, we work with the general theory that if we manage our classrooms well, with clear expectations around student behavior, then discipline will be minimized, and learning will be prioritized. In practice, however, we know that some days, even the best designed disciplinary or management strategies can be completely ineffective, while on other days, these processes may work seamlessly.

Classroom management (including rules, regulations, and routines) typically suggests keeping students quiet (or perhaps we should say somewhat quiet) and orderly, although some of our best classrooms sound the noisiest, appear the most chaotic, and may exhibit rather unconventional, but inspiring and fun, instructional strategies. We understand that noise levels are not the sole indicator of successful classroom management, much like neat rows do not imply that students are absorbing, processing, and properly acting on newly gained knowledge. But for the sake of understanding our concepts, assume that management, for now, implies the classroom is buzzing along without loud screams, crashes, or arguments—in other words, the opposite of what teacher friend Kimi experienced.

After Kimi shared her story of the bee sting and subsequent classroom chaos, we had the opportunity to chat with Ms. Childs, the administrator who entered Kimi's classroom expecting to find an orderly classroom focused on learning math, but instead walked in to chaos. Ms. Childs understood that Kimi's classroom reality in that moment was not the norm. As she explained why classroom management matters and remains something that she looks for while engaging in classroom rounds, this remark struck us:

> My number one need in the school is security. I must be able to trust that my teachers are doing what they need to do to keep everyone safe. If I lose that trust, then I feel as if I've lost my ability to even lead. Too many lives are at stake to ignore the chaos and confusion that can erupt when well managed classrooms turn into unplanned chaos.
>
> (Ms. Childs, administrator)

Others have expressed similar concerns such as "if the classroom is in chaos, how can learning take place?" (Rothstein-Fisch & Trumbull, 2008, p. 1). Ms. Childs acknowledged what many educational researchers and practitioners have previously declared that order ensures an expectation of a safe environment, which in turn promotes student and staff comfort with the environment and thus an improved willingness to embrace the learning process. In other words, order leads to better opportunities to learn, which should imply that our classrooms can be identified as safer and more secure.

Can we say that all of today's students regularly desire to behave in an orderly, logical, and potentially subdued manner? Consider the following:

◆ Websites, including social media sites, are dedicated to posts about the most violent, graphic, and disruptive fights and school-based behaviors students can capture in real time.

- ◆ Students have used social media to capture teachers doing or saying things they disagreed with for the greater purpose of destroying the teacher's career.
- ◆ Many trauma-induced behaviors among today's students can lead to meltdowns, unexpected physical or emotional reactions that may prove disruptive, or apathy.
- ◆ Consider the frequent opportunities students have to post their own singing, dancing, or skateboarding moves to social media because they live in an Internet-connected world that screams for them to be known as influencers (e.g., TikTok or Instagram).

It is normal to expect that this attention-seeking cultural norm that surrounds non-school lives makes itself present in our classrooms, a place where we typically want to minimize the most disruptive, graphic, violent, or attention-seeking behaviors because they can be unsafe and distract from learning.

Managing orderly classrooms with a generation that frequently hears that the way to go "viral" is by doing the unexpected, the uncomfortable, or the most shocking of behaviors, is a challenge. We teach a generation that is constantly connected to music, dance, and all sorts of stimuli on a 24/7 basis, thanks to smartphones, so asking them to put much of that aside to behave well and attend to learning is almost akin to asking an Olympian to never practice his/her sport again. It just goes against the grain, and it makes classroom management hard, if not utterly impossible. It is okay to say that you feel as if you cannot manage your students' out of control, illogical, or unexpected behaviors because, frankly, not many of us can do much better.

Flip the switch for a moment and consider classroom management in a room that is purposefully chaotic. In the interest of creativity and collaboration for the learning process, it is often appropriate to have loud classrooms where student voices all but reverberate through the walls or where desks are never in orderly formations, and classroom supplies and learning tools appear to have no apparent order. As we already said, nice, neat rows of desks with students barely whispering and always saying "yes, ma'am" or "no, sir" does not necessarily equate to well-managed classrooms where students thrive with their learning efforts.

Noise is often necessary to robust debate and creative expression, and there are some culturally driven behaviors that equate louder voices with being noticed. We did not write this chapter to position ourselves as the "noise police," advising you to keep your students from talking above a whisper if you are to be fully identified as a safety-conscious teacher. Please give students a voice, even if it is a loud voice, and let it be their honest voice of expression, so they understand they are valued in the learning community. But. . . .

There is something to be said for managing noise levels so that students can safely hear your instructions and follow key instructions. When behaviors and conversations spiral wildly out of control, we and our students don't feel as safe or secure as we did before it happened. Why? Because there is a hint of the "unknown" in that moment. What's happening? Is this supposed to be happening? That is why a book on safe and secure schools must address classroom management. Mismanaged and misunderstood behaviors or conditions can lead to distress for you and other stakeholders.

Questions for the Reader

Can a loud, active classroom be an indicator of a severely mismanaged classroom? Why or why not? What is your comfort level with a noisy classroom? What does noise in a classroom mean?

Just a Thought: Think about a time when you were asked or forced to radically alter your teaching style or communication practice. Did you perhaps feel a loss of control at that moment? Did you feel a bit helpless and uncomfortable? Reflect on that helplessness and frustration for a moment. The sobering feeling we experience when our world is rocked has to continuously drive us to remember that our students really do need robust classroom management and clear expectations, or else they feel uncomfortable and lost. Chaos rarely leads to improved learning, and you have every right to expect that your students appreciate your ability to manage a room well, a point that now moves us on to the three Rs of safety and security.

Your Comfort and Classroom Management

Maintaining order and safety in a classroom is no small task, and because this task grew increasingly more challenging as schools returned to the actual building following the global pandemic of 2020–2021, with more intense and magnified student behaviors, schools have been left struggling to figure out what sort of approach or framework to use to equitably consider all student behaviors.

In the next few chapters, we will explore some of the more common approaches to classroom management in America's schools today, including frameworks such as positive behavioral interventions and supports (PBIS), restorative justice, and other alternative behavior options that have grabbed headlines and sparked much debate around the question: What is best for our school and for my classroom?

But before we get to the frameworks and options, let's get back to the basics: maintaining safe and secure schools does not start with complicated or expensive behavioral programs, cool rewards or awards, or overwhelming zero-tolerance environments in which students are suspended if they look at somebody the wrong way. Behavioral and disciplinary systems, protocols, and frameworks certainly play an important role, but before all of that fancy stuff, we have to remind ourselves that maintaining safe and secure schools starts with simple, critical procedures and practices that every teacher should embrace from day one in the classroom. If we want safe schools and secure schools, start with the three Rs.

The Three Rs: Rules, Routines, and Regularity

Teacher Tools: Defining the Three Rs
Rules: Classroom or school-wide behavioral, emotional, and learning expectations
Routines: The frameworks and structures within which learning occurs and behavior is expressed and addressed
Regularity: There is predictability around expected classroom or school procedures, and predictable patterns or procedures are only broken when it's in the best interest of all involved or for purposes of improving safety and security

For our highly experienced classroom teacher friends reading this book, you may feel that we are taking you back to a simplistic foundation of knowledge that you have heard thousands of times before. If that is the case, we beg your apologies. Bear with us for just a moment, as we have to build the basics before we advance to the more complicated decisions we face when trying to keep our schools safe and secure.

Friendly Safe School Advice: To keep your classroom, yourself, and the lives of those you serve safe at school, aim to first identify the most critical classroom **rules and routines** to keep everyone focused on pro-social, safe behaviors. In addition, **embrace regularity** so students know what to expect. Even a strong teacher can fail to connect with students if they fail to learn, understand, and embrace the rules and regulations of your local classroom.

We believe if your students know that purposeful learning establishes the core foundation upon which you build connections and a shared sense of classroom community that promotes safety, they will begin to adjust behaviors accordingly. If your students fear what they will encounter each day upon arriving at school, question your predictability, or have concerns about frequent unknowns, then you have got a serious problem before the first bell ever rings. Uncertainty breeds anxiety, which in turn yields to fear and may result in students literally shutting down and refusing to engage in the learning process. Prioritize easing your students' fears by teaching them how to engage in the life of school with carefully identified, pro-social rules and regular patterns of behavior (from making a trip to the cafeteria to an afternoon stretch break).

> Rules and routines keep your class running smoothly so that you have more time for teaching academics.
> (California Teachers Association, 1999, para. 1)

Questions for the Reader

If rules and routines help us create communities of shared understandings, then whose rules do we adopt? There are as many rules and routines out there as flavors of ice cream, so we feel compelled to ask: What sort of rules or whose rules should you embrace in your classroom, and what are you supposed to do if you have the prettiest and most comprehensive rules in town, but your students really don't care and have no intention of ever following the rules? In this chapter, we start with rules. In the next, we explore the real-world reality of apathy toward our rules.

Whose Rules?

Tip #1—Pro-social Rules

Our first tip is to consider adopting pro-social rules that focus on the desired behavior rather than the undesired behavior (e.g., "Be kind" as opposed to "Don't be rude to others"). Framing rules in positive, proactive ways sends a message that these behaviors are welcomed. Prohibitive rules tend to focus more on undesirable behaviors and offer no clear construct of what is practically expected (e.g., If the rule is "no running," then what can I do? Can I walk? Can I skip? Can I hop down the hallway to recess?). Consider these commonly adopted pro-social rules that you may have seen in school classrooms, youth athletic sports teams, or local community centers:

- ◆ Be kind to everyone.
- ◆ Be respectful.
- ◆ Be safe.
- ◆ Be responsible.
- ◆ Be nice.
- ◆ Be thoughtful.
- ◆ Help your neighbor.

Tip #2—Do Not Apologize for Having Rules

Some would argue that rules assume our students want to misbehave and that imposing rules on them will negatively impact their creativity, thought, and exploration of the world. We tend to live in a world today where the construct of absolute rules with punitive consequences is marked as bad or inappropriate for flourishing students. But our learners need to clearly understand what we expect, when we expect it, and how to engage properly and safely. There is nothing wrong with a few rules, and you should never apologize for enforcing them!

Think of rules like seatbelt laws. Seatbelt laws force us to wear seatbelts in the car, which can also be construed as a restriction of movement and freedom. But the laws exist for one core purpose—to protect us in a collision. Similarly, think of classroom rules and regulations as the driving forces that give us a better environment in which to operate so that everyone in our school community is kept safer and feels safer.

Here are some things to think about as you build your set of classroom expectations:

- ◆ Make the expectations clear. (Are they written in student-friendly language? Are they accessible to all students?)
- ◆ Make the expectations relevant. (Do students know why these rules are important?)

- ◆ Make them editable but within certain parameters. (Allow students to provide input into how or why certain rules might interfere with their learning.)
- ◆ Consider how they are perceived by all stakeholders. (Did you gather feedback from other teachers? From parents? From school leaders?)
- ◆ Consider whether they are created by all stakeholders. (Again, what is the role of parents and school leaders in these processes?)
- ◆ Explain them well. (Have an honest conversation with your students often, and not just on the first day of school. Emphasize rules as routines, not randomly enforced events.)
- ◆ Establish a common understanding around each rule. (Apply rules consistently and fairly so that students know what to expect when a rule is violated.)

Successful implementation of classroom rules in any setting requires consistency (this explains the second R, "regularity). If you are inconsistent in how you explain, interpret, or respond to students who violate the rules, which may result in inconsistent consequences or teacher remarks, you only create confusion.

Questions for the Reader

Do you think your students ever feel confused about your classroom expectations or rules? How would you know? What could you do differently to make the rules in your classroom clearer?

Whether you are a pre-service, first year, beginning, or veteran teacher, we offer a friendly reminder to be consistent and at peace with whatever rules you adopt. Be bold and explain to students why you have taken the approach that is best for your classroom learning community. Honestly challenge students to voice how their disruptive behaviors could destroy everything positive that is meant to happen at school. When you feel peace about the approach that works best for you and your learners and it promotes a safer and more secure environment, then you will rest easier, knowing you have taken a critical step to an overall safer and more secure school setting.

Think and Write

Think about this topic in regard to your current classroom and consider using these questions with colleagues:

- ◆ **Question 1:** What are your current classroom rules?
- ◆ **Question 2:** Are your rules largely proactive?
- ◆ **Question 3:** If you don't have classroom rules, how have you managed expectations?
- ◆ **Question 4:** Do you allow input from students, parents, or school leaders in the rules you set for your classroom? Why or why not?

We ask you to investigate these specific questions because they play a role in the type of classroom climate that you ultimately establish for students. Consider how each rule supports or diminishes the safety and security of your classroom.

From Rules to Procedures and Patterns

If rules help students know what is expected in a typical classroom day, thereby ensuring predictability and safety, then procedures and patterns add to this foundation. What is a procedure and how is it different from a rule? Consider these common procedures:

- ◆ Wash your hands before lining up for lunch.
- ◆ Sign out on the clipboard before taking the restroom pass.
- ◆ Check in when you enter the room.
- ◆ Raise your hand if you wish to ask or answer a question.
- ◆ Put your chair on top of your desk before heading out to the buses.

While rules are about our general expectations around how we treat ourselves and other people, procedures help us understand what to do and when to do it. Procedures help students practice routines and expectations around movement and motion in the classroom or school building. Expected procedures, like known rules and regular behaviors, give students (and teachers) an expanded feeling of safety—"I know how I am expected to behave, and if I do what is asked, things will run smoothly." This is particularly true when the procedure is a fire drill, tornado drill, or active shooter drill.

Consider the types of procedures you might ask your students to engage with in the face of an emergency:

♦ Refrain from talking or moving away from windows and doors within your classroom.
♦ Sit in a dark, locked room until given notice that it is safe to exit.
♦ Listen, in silence, as movement occurs outside your classroom.
♦ Adhere to instructions from an unfamiliar teacher or school leader.
♦ Curtail or suspend mobile phone usage.
♦ Physically position oneself differently (under a desk, in a closet, behind a barrier).
♦ Move objects to unique positions in the classroom.
♦ Tend to injuries if they occur.
♦ Manage emotions, adrenaline, and anxiety.
♦ Witness injuries of classmates or teachers.

Trusted patterns of behavior in the face of potential threats to your safety and security at school, including listening critically and understanding where to go or when to go to a safer spot, as identified by the adult in charge, will ease fears and result in more predictable behaviors despite unexpected chaos leading to the unthinkable (e.g., armed intruder; natural disaster strikes the building).

More Than a Teacher

When we reflect on the many procedures that your school or district leadership might expect you to introduce to students, particularly in regards to having a safe and secure school (including everything from how to walk quietly to the cafeteria each day to how to load the bus safely or hide in the classroom when an armed intruder enters the building), then we must acknowledge the multi-faceted role you are embracing when you start to teach. You become a teacher, police officer, hallway monitor, and so much more!

And yet, perhaps we do not think enough about how your multifaceted role as "teacher" impacts our nerves and feelings as human beings. When you signed up to be a teacher, did you realize you were also signing up to manage a crisis, take someone's temperature, or protect students from a tornado?

Your role in a safe, secure classroom, particularly when faced with a real threat to that classroom, is more than that of being a device, lock, or bullet deterrent. Your role during a crisis—whether pretend or real—is instead that of a crisis leader. You must have the right rapport, proper insight, and trust with students and school community members to lead your students or other stakeholders to safety—in whatever way that is. And you cannot build trust with students if they do not respect you and your clearly defined rules, regulations, and regulated procedures to drive a safer and more secure learning environment. Although some might expect a book on safe and secure schools to start with mention of weapons and drills, we firmly believe that safe and secure schools start secure schools start with a foundational level of understanding how we behave and move in the classroom.

While you, in a real crisis, might barricade doors and hunker down in the classroom corner or even physically move a group of students to an entirely different, yet safer, location in or outside of a building, the key is that you are the leader of the crisis at that moment in time to those students. Your voice, your instincts, and your authority should be things they lean on for guidance, but they will never be able to do this if you have not modeled those expected behaviors or procedures well.

Your ability to lead students through the mundane (How do we hang our backpacks in our cubbies? How do we indicate today's lunch choice?) and the morbid (targeted attacks on the buildings, an unexpected death in the building, even by natural causes) is the ultimate answer to how we maintain a safe and secure classroom. Knowing people will listen to you, follow your lead, and respond quickly and efficiently in the face of an emergency will carry your classroom and your school much further in its efforts to being safe than will ensuring that everyone on staff knows how to move the teacher desk in front of the windows for an easier escape.

Establishing Trust With Stakeholders

We believe the most critical factor in maintaining welcoming, inviting, predictable, safe, and secure learning communities is trust; trust between the school community (students, colleagues, school leaders, community members) and among those embracing commonly established norms and procedures.

Establishing relevant classroom rules, routines, and procedures should not be about trying to catch students doing wrong or about highlighting a teacher's power. Most teachers do not find enjoyment in redirecting the student who has chosen to hit her/his classmate or to make inappropriate noises during a read aloud. Most teachers we know would rather deliver rigorous content than spend even 10 seconds correcting anti-social and inappropriate behaviors and/or responding with consequences. Simple, consistent rules can help eliminate some of the undesired behaviors from day one, if handled correctly, although it will never stamp out all misbehaviors.

We should not use our power as teachers to correct anti-social, undesired, or bullying behaviors just because we can. Instead, we should use our position as a classroom leader to establish the necessary foundation of order and to correct potentially dangerous behaviors for purposes of building a deeper trust. Additionally, when coupled with routines and procedures, we keep everyone emotionally and physically safer during the academic day.

It is this bigger purpose that reminds us to engage other school community members in the process. Getting parents, local businesses, non-profits, faith-based groups, and other community members on board with our expectations is key to success. If we build a school community where norms cross the thresholds of the school doors, it is likely our community will be transformed alongside our school rather than despite it.

Teacher Tool

As teachers, we need a path to express our concerns, share our successes, and learn as we become more experienced in our careers. Trust, as a professional trait, is not simply assumed, and there are steps we can take to understand how we need to behave to build and earn the trust of others. To this purpose, we end this chapter with the TRUST acronym—an acronym that reminds us how to use our voices well.

T: Tell others your fears, worries, and needs. Admitting weaknesses does not mean you are an ineffective teacher; rather, it means you are in touch with your emotions enough to know you have human emotions being in the classroom. It helps others understand where development might be needed and where holes exist in our leadership support framework.

R: Remember to empower those around you to take a larger role. When we think of safe and secure classrooms, we are only as safe and secure as our four walls can be. We need those in classrooms, hallways, and learning areas around us to also embrace safe and secure policies and procedures. Ask your colleagues how they are building safe classrooms. Where do they feel weaknesses are present? Who can you go to to get information about safe practices?

U: Understand that leadership does not always have the right answers. When an emergency or crisis happens, we often defer to school leaders to guide our way. However, in many schools, school leaders are frequently dealing with the crisis in a different location or cannot be contacted through school channels. It is at this time that we need to rely on our practiced leadership and trusted relationships with students to carry out plans for safety. In addition, when talking through the what ifs, consider that your school leader may not have spent a great deal of time knowing the intricacies of your classroom or your hallway so you may need to have a shared learning conversation for your school leaders to understand the unique challenges of your particular learning environment.

S: Speak up and speak out: Again, you are the professional with the most knowledge about your learning area. If you see a gap in safety or potential for harm, speak up, alert school leadership, and ensure action is taken.

T: Turn negatives into positive opportunities for partnership: Crises or emergencies always provide a time after the fact to consider what went well and what could have gone better. No emergency is handled perfectly and with each challenge to your classroom's security and safety, you, too, will learn the idiosyncrasies of working with students or within learning environments. Engage in these conversations to openly share what you are seeing, learning, and thinking about regarding your safety and your students' safety. Build partnerships with colleagues, school leaders, and other school personnel so that when a crisis arises, you know you are working as a team, whether you can communicate with each other or not.

Take Action! Ways Teachers Can Take Action to Build Safe and Secure Classrooms

We know teachers are integral in maintaining safe and secure classrooms. But how do we get a seat at the table where decisions are being made? What, specifically, can we do to get involved in the processes that affect our classrooms?

1. Attend school board meetings and any open administrative meeting you can to listen closely for new

policies and suggestions about how schools can be safer or more secure. Ask questions. Share your comments in public. Make it clear that you are a teacher and that you are listening and have something to say.

2. Volunteer, in person and in writing, to serve on school safety committees. Make it known the importance of teacher's voices in these decisions and how inviting teachers to the decision-making process is a wise political and ethical decision for school leaders. If your school safety committee does not have a teacher-member, volunteer to serve in that role so that the committee membership is changed.

3. Document safety and security challenges in your working space. Do not hide deficiencies in safety practices and do not ignore potential security issues. Report any identifiable, real security and safety issue in writing to your school leadership team. Provide documentation like photos or evidence of the lax in your report. Save a copy for your files. Ensure that these issues are addressed. Follow up with your report. Check to make sure things get done. If they do not, reopen the lines of communication to make it clear that to do your job, you need to know safety and security is not compromised.

4. Demand professional development that is humane and compassionate towards all of the school community. If you are told that you are required to participate in professional development that may cause emotional trauma, like those with fake bullets, sounds of hallway shootings, or triage centers, be specific and articulate as to why that type of training is not something you will participate in. This may become a larger issue of insubordination, so prepare yourself with meaningful evidence of how these types of trainings jeopardize teacher mental and emotional health.

5. Uphold the sanctity of school security and safety. That is, do not create shortcuts through evacuation routes, get lax with your hall-monitoring duty, or halfheartedly participate in lockdown drills. If your daily practices show that you really do not care about the integrity of safe and secure school practices, do not expect to be invited to participate in the revision of those practices in the future. Your actions will speak volumes.

Reflective Questions for Teachers and Leaders

1. What behaviors do you want to promote through your classroom policies? To deter?
2. Talk to other teachers. What tone and trends do these policies set? Explore the motivation behind the policies with the teachers.
3. What do you wish your school leader knew about your classroom policies? How can you begin that conversation?
4. When and where do you communicate your daily classroom and unexpected emergency policies or procedures with students and other stakeholders (e.g., parents)?
5. How can you work collaboratively with other teachers to create a consistent learning environment through the policies and practices in your classrooms?

4

Managing Your Classroom Management Technique

As a special education teacher, I was asked to co-teach a biology class. One day I sat next to a student who was focused on doing something else besides her biology assignment, I told her to put that aside to listen to the other classroom teacher, and we would return to it later. She ignored me and finally said what she was doing was far more important than listening to a teacher. She left school that afternoon and went home and told her mom that I had disrespected her. Next thing I know, I'm being called into the principal's office, which was filled with a table of district level administrators. Somehow, I was the one facing trouble because I dared to insist she do her work!

—Demetria, high school special education teacher

Have you, like Demetria, ever faced a challenging behavioral situation, only to feel as if others are pointing at you as the impetus for a student's anti-social behaviors? It is not a positive or enriching situation for anyone involved. It is gut-wrenching, embarrassing, and a complete waste of time. Demetria's story is exactly why we asked in the prior chapter what we are to do when there is nothing but apathy toward our rules, regulations, procedures, and positive supports.

It is extremely difficult for a teacher to face circumstances in which their classroom authority is called into question or investigated in such a way that everything dissolves into a "he said, she said," finger-pointing situation, and the teacher's authority quickly fades away. It is also impossible to walk away from this situation with pride, tears, and anger in check, maintaining a consistent image of professionalism.

DOI: 10.4324/b23214-5

These situations hurt, as they often call into question every-thing we think we know to be true about who we are and why we even teach. Plus, they make us ask: "How did we get here? How did I go from teaching a powerful lesson an hour ago to suddenly feeling as if I am in front of a disciplinary review board with every practice and procedure critiqued like a criminal in custody?" There is a certain amount of emotional frustration that accompanies incidents like this in which we feel inappropriately or unfairly questioned or critiqued, and sadly, it feels as if this has become the norm, rather than the exception, in many of our schools.

What Would You Do?

Put yourself in Demetria's shoes and reflect on how you feel after you exit the principal's office. What emotions are pres-ent? How could she have handled the situation differently? What should she be asking of her administrator? How do you feel and why do you feel this way? Write your thoughts in the space below.

The reason we share Demetria's story is because it forces us to have a critical conversation around classroom management, basic discipline, and our overall expectations. In prior chapters, we established the idea that clear classroom expectations, pro-social rules, and an expectation of regularity in the learning process lay the foundation for establishing a trusting and caring school culture in which the teacher is honored, respected, valued, and safe.

When classrooms dissolve into chaos, when no one seems to know what to expect or how to function, then an unsafe, insecure condition can become reality for students and teachers. That is why we address the difficult topic of "discipline" and expected or unexpected school behaviors, starting with the teacher's role in setting the tone and leading success with all things discipline.

Schools frequently adopt disciplinary systems or frameworks for the purpose of having a clearly understood system within which to respond to unwanted and antisocial behaviors. But there are many systems on the market, which lead to the question: What is the best system to make sure my student behaviors pose no threat to our overall safety and security?

Because behavioral concerns can differ from classroom to classroom, from school to school, and from state to state, there is no "one-size-fits all" solution to classroom management, discipline, and safety. We must never forget that even a district with 100 schools is facing 100 unique school cultures, and what works at one may not work at another. But frameworks and protocols can help us promote positive cultures, and the teacher's voice in making these decisions is key.

In this chapter, we dive into commonly adopted disciplinary and behavioral frameworks that schools have utilized to promote safe, secure, inclusive environments. But before we do, here are a few key principles:

- ◆ Intense behavior issues that occur among students identified under the special education umbrella (often as a manifestation of a disability) are unique, and the way in which we address and manage those concerns must be in compliance with what is appropriate for the student and aligned with their Individual Education Program (IEP).
- ◆ No student behavior that is physically or mentally damaging to students and staff should be tolerated or ignored. Again, you should never be exposed to unsafe behaviors.
- ◆ It is not acceptable for teachers, administrators, other staff, or students to be physically harmed, and every effort must be made to minimize potential harm that emerges from student actions.
- ◆ We must make every effort to understand how our personal and professional biases and experiences may impact how we approach discipline.

♦ If selected disciplinary frameworks leave staff believing that students lack consequences for behaviors, then the selected framework can never work effectively. There must be active dialogue about the construct of "consequence" and what is acceptable or not acceptable.

♦ Promoting equitable, safe, and secure conditions and consequences for potentially harmful behaviors is not a reason to ignore behaviors that put individuals at risk of harm.

♦ Trauma-induced behaviors that endanger your safety are to be minimized.

Consider why teachers today feel like they are blamed for, or identified as the cause of, student misbehaviors—a common thread of discussion among the media, parents, and students alike.

Blaming Teachers, Building Dialogue

Teacher testimonies reveal that many, like Demetria, have felt questioned and belittled and had their authority overturned in disciplinary matters involving angry parents who complained that the teacher was too strict with their child or that their child was treated unfairly. The result? Devastated, depressed, and stunned teachers who dare to ask, "Why do I even bother, and why is his/her misbehavior my fault?" Consequently, many have chosen to leave the profession. In any given week, you can turn to social media to find a very frustrated teacher who explains something like this . . .

The kids don't care. They don't respect me. Nobody holds them accountable for anything. I'm so over it. Why do I bother?

If we are to keep our schools and districts as safe and secure as possible, then the last thing we need is disappointed, overwhelmed teachers who wonder why they bother to show up, care for kids, or respond with patience in extreme conditions. You likely know teachers who have given up enforcing rules or following school procedures because of their frequent experiences of being undermined or questioned in a way that implied they were wrong.

Studying education for the past few decades, we have seen a significant shift around issues of right and wrong—not in an existential way but in terms of what we admit is appropriate or inappropriate for school conduct. Just a few decades ago, students were facing school discipline for having long hair or for violating school dress codes. It was once unthinkable that students might assault each other on an almost daily basis or even think about bringing (and using!) a weapon to school, yet now we have websites dedicated to the full-time display of recorded school assaults, breaking news about school resource officers who discovered a gun or knife in a student's backpack, parents who assaulted an educator in public, or classroom fights that sent three students to the hospital.

Does this imply we are now okay with this aggressive and dangerous student and external stakeholder behavior, to the point that we tell worried teachers that this is just the way things are today, so accept it?

Disclaimer: We fully understand and acknowledge that teachers are wrong at times and can, like their students, turn into perpetrators, guilty of harassing or bullying others. In fact, there are ample examples of teachers bullying fellow teachers (Kelmon, 2014). The title of teacher does not imply perfection, nor does it indicate that we always know the best decision to make in the face of threats or frustration.

We enter the teaching profession with different levels of training and preparation around classroom and school-based management processes, including our understanding of the type of responses that are allowable or acceptable. For this reason, we approach this chapter about classroom management and school expectations with caution.

From the school leader viewpoint, we know how difficult it can be to remove a tenured teacher who fails to meet expectations, belittles students, or refuses to adhere to school procedures and policies. Things are messy and difficult when school leaders feel disappointed with a teacher's conduct or when a teacher feels under attack by the administration for their behaviors.

We understand school and district administrators carry a heavy burden when faced with challenging teacher personnel issues, particularly when it involves teacher on teacher hostility, disgruntled teachers who feel disempowered, or emotionally unwell teachers who respond with unexpected behaviors. School leadership is not exactly a comedy club experience, particularly when a teacher's frustration leads them to make an unwise or hostile response that somehow goes viral. Thus, we acknowledge that teachers, counselors, social workers, bus drivers, and everyone else involved in the world of schooling our youth can make unwise decisions in the heat of the moment. We are human after all.

But if we return to the idea that teachers often feel accused or blamed for select student behaviors that they did not provoke (which is a common theme among our personal teacher friends), then we must say we are alarmed at what appears to be an increasingly hostile dialogue that points fingers at teachers. We sense an implied argument that teachers really do not like those they teach and are assuming the role of jail warden, with a desire to inflict the most painful or worst punishment on students they dislike.

It has frankly become far too easy to blame teachers for the problems in schools today, particularly around unwanted and anti-social behaviors (e.g., He only attacked you because you pushed him too hard to engage in learning), while ignoring the need to sit down and have a difficult conversation around why it is so easy to point fingers in that direction, a solution that ultimately does not solve anything.

Coupled with teacher concerns about accepting blame for student misbehaviors is teacher frustration with school or district attempts to make the guilty students look better on paper, which in turn makes school and district records more amenable to public approval. There is no lack of headlines about the way select schools or districts have unfortunately doctored data, at times, when under pressure to make attendance and graduation rates look stronger and disciplinary charges appear minimal (Grossman, 2015; Jones, 2018; Strauss, 2015).

What Would You Do?

Imagine for a moment that you are a teacher in a district that you believe has failed to accurately identify or respond to potentially dangerous, threatening, or disruptive student behaviors. You've seen this often with one of your eighth grade students who repeatedly yells out expletives, shoves others' desks, and mimics or mocks you when you are teaching. You've sent him to see the principal three times in two weeks but have learned that each time he visited the main office, he was seen riding around on the school "Gator" with the head football coach helping to paint stripes on the field for Friday night's big football game.

What do you do? Do you speak up, and if you do, what do you say? If this selected response to student behavior means you and your other students are safe, then is it ok to allow the student to "help" a staff member with athletic duties?

Doctored Books or Desperate Decisions

Are all schools blaming teachers for every student's misbehavior? Are school or district leaders regularly doctoring the books around violent, dangerous, or attendance behaviors? Are leaders systemically ignoring all behaviors that may be physically harmful for fear that they will be viewed as too harsh?

The short answer is "no." We make no attempt to imply that this is regular or "to be expected" practice. But we know the following to be true:

◆ It is too easy to blame teachers for triggering student behaviors, avoiding an exploration of root cause analysis that will reveal the real trigger.
◆ It is similarly too easy to blame school leaders for failing to issue effective consequences for anti-social or harmful

student behaviors when the reality is that no consequence can fully address the root cause of behavior.

♦ At times, school leaders choose to exercise "alternative consequences" for intense classroom behaviors because they have no other choice—their hands are tied, and they feel pressure to reduce punitive responses to extreme behaviors.

♦ At times, student behaviors stem from mental health concerns that frankly no school disciplinary system can resolve, leaving the administrator in a situation of doing what makes everyone happy or doing what keeps people immediately safe.

♦ The impact of trauma-induced antisocial behaviors leaves all of us wondering what to do at times. There is no easy "one size fits all" when trauma is the trigger.

With this said, we have two options if we are going to effectively address harmful or anti-social student behaviors that put persons at risk: (1) we give up and assume there is no good response, meaning schools continue to crumble into chaos, or (2) we consider systems currently in place at schools around the nation and reflect on how they might impact our local learning community. Your authors advocate for finding a system that works for you and your students, understanding that even the best system cannot address many of the more alarming behaviors experienced in schools today.

Finding a System that Works

A discipline plan for a classroom, school, or district is grounded in identifying rules, norms, procedures, and patterns of behavior. When expectations are clear, behaviors generally improve. When responses are consistent and reinforced by the school community, a culture is built. This does not mean that things do not go wrong or that our adopted disciplinary frameworks cannot stand a little improvement.

Today's schools appear to have greater options for disciplinary frameworks than did schools of a few decades ago. Most schools have the option to select from a more traditional disciplinary framework (broken rules = punishment or punitive consequences) or a modern or alternative disciplinary framework that takes either a strengths-based or an alternative consequences approach. Consider the pros and cons of a more traditional disciplinary framework.

Traditional Discipline

Traditional disciplinary frameworks start with a set of rules associated with specific consequences. If you break the rules, you are subject to a consequence (or punishment). It is often built on an inflexible, firm system of commonly adopted truths around what is right or wrong in a classroom or school setting and explicit punishments are issued for behaviors deemed wrong or unsafe. Think of these frameworks as zero-tolerance policies.

Sample consequences are not limited to but may include:

♦ Detention
♦ Out-of-school suspension
♦ Expulsion
♦ Removal of recess time
♦ Saturday school

Penalties and punishments are meant to reinforce the importance of the rule and to build motivation for a student to avoid breaking the rules again. Traditional disciplinary frameworks operate under a deterrence system of thinking—that is, if a student is considering violating a rule, knowing the potential penalty might deter the student from breaking the rule in the first place.

Specific to attendance concerns, if students under a traditional disciplinary system accumulate three school tardies, they receive a predetermined number of days of lunch or after-school detention. With increased tardies, students transition from in-school to out-of-school suspensions. A system like this with increasing levels of severe punishment is a traditional, predictable system that is frequently detailed in a school-wide handbook or plastered across "Rules" posters in local classrooms.

In prior generations, some penalties even took the form of corporal punishment, including acts like spanking, paddling, and public embarrassment, which surprisingly, are still allowed in some states today. But whatever form it comes in, traditional discipline tends to be designed around the notion that punishments will motivate students to act differently in the future or to prevent a behavior altogether.

Many schools today continue to use a traditional disciplinary system because it is (1) easy to understand, (2) easy to determine consequences; and (3) leaves everyone with the clear message that a punitive consequence has been issued for anti-social or harmful behaviors. Traditional disciplinary systems are grounded in firm rules, and as you may recall, we said in the prior chapter that rules are good because they clarify expectations (no gray areas), and it is okay to enforce your rules.

But many schools have started to move away from these systems or are adopting modified systems because (1) they are inflexible, (2) there is no alternative consequence for conditions when it appears the normal punishments will not impact behavior, (3) these traditional systems appear to place diverse student populations at greater risk of punishment, and (4) there is a growing belief that alternative approaches to behavior promote a positive school culture.

Think and Write

Consider these questions about traditional disciplinary models. Where do your experiences lie within this type of system? Use the space to share your written reflections.

1. Would you say that your classroom uses a traditional disciplinary model? If yes, what makes it fit this description?
2. What positive results can happen through traditional discipline models?
3. What negative results may occur as a result of traditional discipline models?

4. Think back to your days as a student in school. Did your teachers use a traditional disciplinary model? What do you remember about it? How effective do you think it was?
5. Is there any part or feature of your current traditional discipline system that you don't care for? What is it?

Non-traditional Discipline

Recent shifts involving greater attention to and significant calls for improved, equitable classroom attention to the social-emotional needs of students include building emotional resilience, addressing student-based trauma, and providing safe environments within which students can work to control intense feelings of rage or anger have led many schools to replace a more traditional disciplinary model with new models of and strategies for behavior modification and development. If your classroom or school adopts a disciplinary framework that is broader than the traditional model and utilizes alternative, previously unimagined behavioral interventions, then it is possible that you have adopted one of these frequently embraced modern frameworks:

◆ PBIS is described as "an evidence-based three-tiered framework for improving and integrating all of the data, systems, and practices affecting student outcomes every day" (Center on PBIS, 2022, para. 1). In a PBIS framework, outcomes from implementation of the support system are personalized to the needs of each school. School leaders are empowered with data, interventions, and strategies to address student behaviors, desired outcomes, and long-term teaching practices for all students.

◆ Trauma-informed care and trauma-informed schools are schools that recognize that students and adults within a school may be impacted by traumatic stress. Schools that embrace these practices acknowledge the reality that trauma can impact everyone and showing up to school does not reduce the magnitude of that impact. Traumas can be from a variety of sources or events and might include things like bullying, the death of a loved one, chronic health problems, living in a violent neighborhood, or even sexual or physical abuse. These practices, then, present a supportive environment with clear expectations and streamlined communication strategies to help anyone in the school community cope with stressful situations (Centers for Disease Control and Prevention [CDC], Infographic, 2022).

◆ Restorative justice promotes problem-solving practices among students. A 2015 article described restorative justice as "bring(ing) students together in peer-mediated small groups to talk, ask questions, and air their grievances" (Davis, 2015, para. 2). Rather than focus solely on behavior issues, restorative justice promotes a community of dialogue wherein adults and students engage in a conflict resolution process, a reconciliatory goal, and a specific reintegration plan for students who have been removed from the school.

As you know from experience, no one behavioral support framework has solved every problem in today's schools. In fact, each approach has its own pros and cons. PBIS is sometimes challenged for its potential misuse of rewards as a means of motivating students to behave well, while restorative justice is criticized for its extensive up-front training requirements and for requiring aggressors and victims to face each other in restorative circles that leave many educators feeling like students faced no consequences for anti-social and sometimes dangerous behavior. Trust me when we say we understand both sides of the arguments for and against each of these potential frameworks.

The point here is that there is no one-size-fits-all answer, and sometimes, the best solution is a merged framework with features from multiple systems. We must embrace this truth as reality and stop searching for the one magic potion. As teachers, we are called on to make decisions utilizing whatever behavior management framework happens to be in place at the school in which we work.

We know that throughout our careers, we will see different approaches to student management ebb and flow, and our job is to not only remain educated, but also to exercise our professional judgment in ways that support the students with whom we work. And we need you to remember that whenever your school's adopted disciplinary framework really is not working well, you must have the boldness to speak up and speak out. With conditions the way they are today, the brutal reality of schooling is that almost no disciplinary framework works that well when students appear to need both academic and intense mental health interventions at the same time.

Question for the Reader

Do you recognize these frameworks, and does your school or classroom utilize any of these approaches currently?

In the meantime, consider this summary of markers of non-traditional disciplinary frameworks:

- The models often focus on building strengths (positive, anti-social behaviors) rather than highlighting weaknesses (anti-social, breaking the rules).
- Alternative actions are taken in response to breaking the rules. For example, instead of receiving a penalty that impedes on a student's freedom like detention or suspension for excessive absences, the school holds a collaborative student–parent conference to identify manageable ways to change habits that might be interfering with school attendance.
- Responses to behavior challenges may also include formal referrals to mental health professionals. For example, students displaying intense anger and engaging in frequent classroom disruptions may benefit from mental

health interventions that introduce the student to age-appropriate coping mechanisms for emotional resiliency.

◆ Restorative justice frameworks put the task of identifying consequences for undesired behaviors back into the hands of the students. This is intended to have the student understand the magnitude of an action and how it affects the school and classroom community and to allow the student some choice in selecting the appropriate response for his or her lack of compliance with community expectations.

In short, non-traditional disciplinary approaches embrace the idea that traditional strategies and behaviors do not work well for all students, especially in cases when trauma, illness, or other mental health issues may result in a student embracing frequent anti-social or unsafe behaviors.

Questions for the Reader

Has your school or district embraced a non-traditional disciplinary framework with alternative consequences for students? If so, what works well? What challenges are there? How is this type of framework supporting a safe and secure school environment?

Assessing Alternative Approaches

Based on our understanding of the pros and cons of alternative frameworks and through dialogue with educators, there are distinct reasons why many schools have opted to put traditional disciplinary frameworks aside to embrace alternative frameworks involving less punitive consequences.

Reasons include (1) alternative systems offer greater flexibility to address individual behaviors; (2) alternative systems appear to promote trust and compassion at a greater level than do traditional systems that feel impersonal and rigid; (3) alternative frameworks give perpetrators the opportunity to seek forgiveness from those he/she has wronged, thereby building stronger trust among students; and (4) alternative frameworks open the door to more equitable responses to diverse behaviors.

But in similar fashion, there are schools that will never embrace alternative approaches, for the exact opposite reason why many have embraced frameworks like restorative justice. Some educators feel that alternative approaches do not issue specific consequences for harmful or rude behaviors, they leave teachers feeling victimized, and they open the door to students feeling as if they can behave without consequences.

In speaking with educators who have worked within alternative frameworks, one common theme that emerged was the notion of poor implementation, meaning alternative frameworks or approaches were often poorly understood by those being asked to embrace them, and this led to nothing but constant confusion and frustration. This insight begs the question: "Can a hybrid model of disciplinary frameworks best fit school needs?" or "Have alternative frameworks failed to convince many teachers of their effectiveness because of issues around implementation?"

Research supports the need for a flexible, teacher-built behavior management system, as Hannigan and Hannigan (2016) indicate that traditional discipline systems do not always work for all students. Additionally, some research (Lacoe & Steinberg, 2019) suggests that the more traditional consequence of out-of-school suspensions can hinder academic progress while not really impacting behaviors. Suffice it to say, there are grounds for revising school frameworks to include a broader base of responses (both traditional and non-traditional).

Some school leaders have taken to refusing to assign out of school suspensions at all (a component of more traditional frameworks), rationalizing that having a student out of school, on the streets, in an unsafe home environment, or sitting in front of a TV all day is contrary to the goals of learning set forth by the school system. And we agree. When students see suspension as a gift, then what have we really accomplished? This opens the door to non-traditional frameworks.

But Barshay (2019) reminds us that the most rigorous argument for restorative justice in 2014 (to address equitable conditions with matters of behavior) is slowly starting to fade in light of more current research showing trendy disciplinary frameworks just aren't working that well either. The newer, trendier, and more equitable approaches lack resounding outcomes around safe, secure, and equitable schools, and their perceived lack of "holding students accountable" is driving higher levels of teacher frustration.

Putting all cards on the table, we firmly believe that no hybrid system will work well unless the hybrid solution includes a rather intense, cooperative mental health arm to address the more violent, volatile, and intense behaviors from students. No system outside of direct mental health support can truly address trauma-induced behaviors or intense anger that leads students to respond to all conditions in anger and with rage. But outside of significant community financial investments, how is this component of a hybrid solution ever possible?

We encourage you to do your homework to stay engaged in the local conversation about discipline. Research disciplinary options with leadership as you become an extension of school leadership. Consider the pros and cons of the framework being implemented in your school. Read articles and information that report the pros and cons of any behavior management plan. Anticipate barriers to implementation early. And realize that confirmed consequences do not always fix behaviors. Be open to addressing severe behaviors requiring mental health support and be open to creative community partnerships that may be needed to fully provide a comprehensive and workable response.

Finally, speak up. If you are able, participate in conversations about how and why your school's behavior management plan is working or failing. Share what you see and experience on a daily basis in your classroom. Be sure school leaders, parents, and students are participants in the conversation about how student conflicts, challenges, and miss-steps will be handled before issues become chronic.

Teacher Tools: Questions for Helping You Identify and Adopt a Workable Classroom Management System

- ◆ What is my role in preventing classroom management issues or meltdowns?
- ◆ What am I afraid to do in regard to classroom management? Why?
- ◆ How will others perceive my classroom management? Why does it matter?
- ◆ When do outsiders (parents, school leaders, counselors) need to be involved in my classroom management?
- ◆ What behaviors have I seen that prevent students from learning?
- ◆ Where have I failed with classroom management?
- ◆ In what areas is my classroom management strong?
- ◆ What do students say about my classroom management? How do I know?
- ◆ As a learner, what interfered with my learning as a student?
- ◆ What do you think is the most common complaint about management issues in your classroom?
- ◆ How is your classroom different from those in your school that have exceptional classroom management skills?
- ◆ How is your classroom different from those in your school that have poor classroom management skills?
- ◆ What is the purpose of your classroom rules? How do students know what the rules and consequences are? When are they reminded?
- ◆ What is your attitude towards classroom management? If it's negative, why is that? What can be done to produce a more optimistic view?
- ◆ How do your own biases impact how you treat students and address behavior?

Demetria's Story Continued

As we bring this chapter to a close, let's return to Demetria's classroom and consider a disciplinary situation that left her shaken. High school student Eddie arrived mid-way through the year to Demetria's school and classroom, only to be caught with marijuana in his possession three days later. He was suspended, as would be the likely outcome of a traditional disciplinary framework, and returned to school but with sporadic absences because of three out-of-school-time arrests requiring court appearances.

In fact, one day Eddie stood up in the middle of a test, said, "I've got to go to court," and out the door he went with no further explanation. Eddie was rarely in school for the remainder of this semester, but somehow, he earned enough credits to graduate.

Demetria ended the year frustrated. It was two more years until retirement, but she was not sure she could endure another 24 months. How did a student known to carry drugs on campus, skip class, and rarely engage in anything that resembled learning gain promotion and academic credits?

Can any behavioral system respond to this reality well, when it appears that the first thing Eddie needs is highly focused mental health support with counseling and intense interventions? Probably not. That's why we encourage schools to stay flexible and realize that even traditional behavioral systems today need to be partnered with a compassionate mental health resources that helps address the bigger root causes of dangerous behaviors; although few schools have this capacity because they are, after all, schools, and not mental health hospitals.

Take Action! Ways Teachers Can Take Action to Build a Larger Conversation around Classroom Management

Consider the following actions to improve school-based conversations and evoke change around classroom management and school behavior processes:

1. Accurately report and document student behaviors that interfere with learning. While most documentation

requires a retelling of events and is most likely to ensure a student receives adequate notice of how and when a behavior violation has taken place, use any available space on the form to indicate how and why student learning was impacted. So rather than "Jesse interrupted class," be specific and indicate how and why Jesse's interruption stopped student learning, caused a delay in reaching classroom learning goals, and impacted others.

2. Redesign the paperwork used in your school to more adequately reflect the goals of the behavior management plan. Again, rather than focus on retelling events, which is necessary, ask for and assign space specifically for the teacher's input.

3. Visit other classrooms specifically to observe classroom management practices to see how fellow teachers manage the students in your school.

4. Be honest about the problems in your classroom. Share specific events and details with your school leader. Hiding problems because you believe they make you look weak or unprepared reduces your professionalism.

5. Request time on school staff meeting agendas specifically to address school-wide behavior goals.

6. Urge school leaders to document how and why they utilize specific disciplinary or management methods.

7. Insist on having adequate materials, resources, and time to manage students, including recommended accommodations, staff assistance, and social support that may be required for challenging situations.

8. Utilize reflective practices to center and control your emotional reactions to management issues.

9. Report abusive, unwelcomed, or illegal behaviors to the proper authorities. If your school leader asks you to ignore or minimize these types of behaviors, protect yourself first and report the behaviors to local law enforcement.

10. Stand up for yourself by prioritizing student learning. It is hard for anyone to argue that you are irratio-
nal or too emotional if your argument for a peaceful,
safe classroom is based on your desire to facilitate
student learning. Use this as the center of your rationale for all behavior management practices.

Reflective Questions for Teachers and Leaders

1. How would you define "discipline" for your classroom or your school? Is it similar or different from
   "management"? How and why?
2. If you currently utilize or previously embraced a
   non-traditional approach to classroom behavioral
   management or discipline, how did that work for
   you and your school?
3. Do you struggle with fairness? Why or why not?
4. How can you better understand the impact of cultural, socioeconomic, and other types of diversity in
   relation to classroom management practices?
5. In what ways do your own biases impact your classroom management practices?

5

Building a Caring Classroom

Everything about classroom management, discipline, and safe schools stems from relationships, and if you can build relationships and have caring connections with students, they are going to want to respond positively when you try to help them redirect their behaviors. It doesn't mean they will be perfect, but knowing you care makes a big difference in some difficult conversations.

—Leslie, first grade teacher

When we think about modern schools, many words come to mind: curriculum, content, courses, campus, students, career and college ready. But the word carrying the most weight is often curriculum. After all, if we are not providing standards-aligned curriculum or content, then one might question why we even bother to teach in the first place.

Our students deserve and should expect rigorous, equitable teaching with instructional strategies that allow each student the opportunity to acquire and personalize content in a way that best fits their learning needs. But behind the curricular planning are real people with hearts, souls, and minds, who cannot expertly deliver content if they are in crisis, much like our students cannot learn and thrive in the classroom if they are in crisis. Schools are places where people need to be cared for, and this includes the students and staff—not to the point that we water down the content to focus exclusively on feelings but to the point that people know others understand and value their challenges and struggles.

In this chapter, we shift from rules, regular expectations, and disciplinary consequences to embrace the concept of care, which

DOI: 10.4324/b23214-6

serves as the bedrock of all decisions we make about disciplinary frameworks and classroom expectations. To have optimal safe and secure schools, we must begin with care—care for ourselves, care for others, and care for the overall purpose of schooling—to grow young minds.

Questions for the Reader

Have you ever been accused of not caring by a student? How did that make you feel at the time? What led up to the situation? How do your students know you care about them? Are there things you do that might make them question how much you care about them?

There is an oft-repeated quote that nobody seems to know how to cite. Some say the original words came from President Theodore Roosevelt. Others attribute it to motivational guru John Maxwell. But either way, if you are in education, you have likely heard this quote: **students do not care how much you know until they know how much you care**.

Teachers often enter the teaching profession out of a passion to teach—to impart knowledge—and to change lives by helping students make learning connections and apply transferable skills to daily living. But even beginning teachers do not have to work many months before realizing that some students do not wish to learn, and it is largely because they claim they do not care. In some cases, they even believe the teacher does not care about them. It might be tempting to say, "Yeah, yeah, whatever" and move past this false student assumption, but we must consider the negative impact of a learner who sincerely believes the educational staff does not care that they exist or whether they learn. And if this idea persists, it can ultimately do more harm than good.

Research shows one of the most important influences on a student's educational experience is the presence of a caring relationship with a teacher (Zakrzewski, 2012). Thus, caring is more than a feel-good side effect of being in school; it also has a direct impact on how much and how meaningful a student's learning is over time. It is a spirit of care that leads us to develop the type of pro-social, affirmative, and explicit rules or classroom procedures that we referenced in Chapter 4, as we know that students seek structure and a clear classroom process will always support, rather than hinder, learning.

Classrooms as Communities of Care

To develop optimal safe, secure, and positive learning environments for learners, we need to maintain a consistent focus on classrooms as "communities of care," places where students want and need to be cared for. Teachers, counselors, administrators, mental health specialists, and other school stakeholders also want and need to be cared for. But as you may be thinking to yourself right now, this is not a bold, new concept. We are not the first educators to argue about communities of care, nor did we originate this concept.

From Starratt's (2004) emphasis on fostering ethical schools through the ethic of care to Nel Noddings' deep exploration of what it means to care for people in schools, "care" is not a new construct in the educational sector, although it may be a construct we struggle to execute well in practice or to even expect for our sanity and security at school. It is easy to say we "care about teaching," "we care about the kids," or "we care about the community," but when students make life in our classrooms challenging or act in a threatening, deeply confrontational manner in our presence, care rapidly dissolves into a crisis, and the only thing we care about in that moment is survival.

As experienced educators, we have known and worked with many teachers who have focused well on creating a "community of care" classroom. Examples include:

- A second grade teacher keeps crackers and other snacks in her desk drawer for students who have not been eating at home and cannot focus on schoolwork.
- An 11th grade science teacher realizes his student, Song, repeatedly enters the first block with no heavy coat

despite outside temperatures of 10 degrees or below. Over the weekend, the teacher purchases a heavy coat and gives it to Song at the end of class on Monday.

◆ A special education inclusion teacher knows one of the young ladies she serves is heartbroken over her parents' divorce. This student arrives at school one day sobbing and distraught. The teacher writes her a pass to be allowed to enter class a few minutes late so she can compose herself in the bathroom.

◆ A fifth grade teacher knows that Miguel, one of his male students, comes from an undocumented family, and his father is on the verge of being sent back to their home country. Miguel has not been able to focus for a week. While on the playground, the teacher initiates a conversation to ask if the young man wants to chat about anything bothering him.

◆ A kindergarten teacher recommends three families for a special community-based Christmas gift-giving program, as she knows the parents are unable to afford gifts

◆ When a seventh grade social studies teacher had to go running out of the building to the hospital to check on her injured teenage son, her next-door colleague wrote lesson plans and taught students in partnership with her own classes.

These are just a few of the stories of care that we know about, and you could likely add your own novel full of additional examples based on your teaching experiences and that of colleagues in your building. We imagine almost everyone reading this book could raise a hand saying they have paid for a student's lunch or field trip expense, bought snacks for a hungry student, have paid for a student's cap and gown, or offered to send a backpack of food home to a family because the parents lost their jobs and have no steady income. And in many cases, we have done these things for students who have used profanity with us, threatened us, or made our classroom life hard. As teachers, we just seem to care because we know we're working with real people with real needs, and real needs must be met before we can learn. Teachers, it seems, compose one of the most generous professions when it comes to caring for others.

Think and Write

Consider a time when you showed care to a student or to his/her family by going the extra mile and meeting a need that you did not have to address. How did it make you feel? Why do you think you exhibited that level of care, and how do you think ignoring that need might have impacted that student's experience in school? Use this space to write about these experiences

Switch gears and consider times when it has been extremely difficult to care for students in your classroom. Maybe you were struggling to understand the student's culture, history, philosophies, traditions, behaviors, language, or personality quirks. And maybe the student was struggling with the same in regard to her/his approach with you. As a result, you seemed constantly at odds with the learner, or she/he believed you sincerely did not care—did not want to help—and preferred other students more. How did that make you feel?

Caring for students is critical, but exhibiting care when confronted with the crass, disrespectful, condescending, and even dangerous behaviors that sadly have become more mainstream in today's classrooms is nearly impossible, which further challenges our ability to exhibit equitable responses in real-world settings. As teachers, we are asked to care even when our heart and mind screams out that we cannot care because our students threatened us, attacked us, or diminished our reputation with vengeful actions and words. And to that we ask: Really? Why should we care when we are under attack, under distress, or treated with blatant disrespect?

Nothing inside of us wants to care when we are attacked. Too many teachers often feel like the battered victim who must smile and say: "I am fine!" despite the daily physical, social, or emotional beatings that rear their heads in many formats today. And to that reality we want to remind you that no, you do not have to care for abusive conditions. You do not have to love being challenged, and you do not have to give in to every student's whims to promote an equitable learning environment. We are teachers; not punching bags, and building an environment of respectful care runs two ways. We should always expect the same in return, so sometimes our "care" demands fine lines of demarcation for optimal safety and sanity, and you are not a bad teacher when you define these lines.

The result of a properly functioning classroom-based community of care will be the building of a classroom environment where student voices are valued, learning takes place, and students will listen to teachers in moments of crisis or concern because they understand the teacher is caring for their overall safety and security. As teachers, we must learn to advocate, ask for, and implement resources to demonstrate our classrooms are classrooms while simultaneously advocating for conditions that promote self-care.

But take a step back for a moment to affirm we share a common understanding of this construct of care. Care and compassion are the foundation of solid personal and professional relationships. We build trusting relationships when we believe people care about us and for us. And nothing could be more critical to establishing safe and secure schools than grounding all of our efforts in this sort of trusting relationship. After all, how can we expect students to follow us to safe shelter in the face of a real tornado preparing to hit the school if they do not even trust us enough to let us read their homework or talk about a failing grade? So, if we are going to agree, at least for a few moments, that care is a critical building block of safe and secure schools, it is important that we share a common understanding of the word.

The Meaning of Care

What is "care?" Have you ever stopped to consider this question? If you are like us, we are far too busy most days dealing with emails, work stress, and personal challenges to honestly sit and reflect deeply on the real meaning of care (outside of giving someone a hug, bandaging a boo-boo, or preparing a meal for a grieving family), but stop for a moment to reflect on "care" as a living, breathing construct that shapes how we do life.

Care is actually many things and manifests itself in unique forms. "Care" can be both a noun and a verb. The noun "care" means the attention you give someone or something (for example, "our priority is the care of our students"). The verb "care" means to look after or provide for someone or something (for example, "I care about your learning"). Used in either form, it is the idea or process of looking after, providing for, tending to, watching over, keeping safe, or maintaining a responsibility over. One dictionary explains care as the provision of things that are "necessary" for health, wealth, and well-being.

We love that concept: providing what is necessary for the well-being of others. That is why we have to address this construct in this book. If keeping kids safe is what is in their best interest, then showing care in a manner that builds a student's ability to trust you, even in the face of threat or risk of harm, is an absolutely critical tool in our teacher toolkit.

Ideally, caring is a part of our presence in the classroom and not an additional duty or something extra to add to your daily to-do list. It is rather innate and often flows out of us to those we serve. Ideally, caring teachers are consistent in their care.

But we admit that some teachers struggle with the challenges of care, asserting: "I'm here to teach—not to wipe noses, hand them tissues when they get dumped by their boyfriend, or give counsel to their friendship spats." Certainly, even among the teaching ranks, we disagree to what extent and to what measure our caring should extend. When does our caring *need* to stop, and when *should* it stop? Or, to put it another way, when does our attempt to care for our students represent overbearing methods, and when does caring place us in a near victim mode of giving in to behaviors that put us or others at risk? Finally, when does caring for our students run the risk of establishing disillusionment around why we do what we do?

A teacher can get overwhelmed when he/she realizes they spent quality time in a teacher preparation program and in gaining expertise in a particular discipline or grade level, only to land their dream job and realize they spend more time caring for daily student crises that hinder instruction than they do imparting content. Consider this beginning teacher's predicament.

What Would You Do?

Benita is a second year math teacher at an inner-city high school serving a highly diverse student body of whom 85% receive free and reduced lunch. Benita is regularly overwhelmed by the physical, financial, and social-emotional needs of her students. Lately, many of her juniors and seniors have been talking about wanting to go to prom this year, but many cannot afford it. They lack semi-formal clothing; cannot pay for the $85.00 entry tickets; and have no way to fund a dinner date, hair, or nail appointment.

Benita mentions this financial concern while at lunch with seven other teachers from the math department, suggesting they start a prom dress fund or collect pre-owned suits and dresses for students to pick from. As Benita continues to explain how widespread the need is, a veteran colleague harshly responds: "Benita, why are you so worried about this? Listen, this is just the way it is. Many of our students' families lack the funds to pay for prom, and you are not their mother. You cannot fix all of their needs, so stop caring and just teach math!"

> **Questions:** What would you do in this moment, and do you think that Benita's efforts to care have gone too far? What possible solutions are there to this issue? How should Benita handle the conflict with her colleagues?

For Benita, meeting the physical and financial needs of her students outside of class was as critical as teaching mathematical skills well. But for other teachers, Benita's level of care felt like an overreach and as something that frankly lies outside of their contract. But care doesn't always have to involve money or the acquisition of things. Consider common ways we show care to students in our classrooms, as actions speak louder than words.

See the table that follows. How many of these ways to show care have been realized in your classroom?

Ways to Show Care in the Classroom

Physically	Emotionally	Academically
Providing ample room to learn	Encouraging students to share frustrations	Providing opportunities to practice new concepts
Ensuring access to resources	Allowing freedom to explore	Accurately assessing student work
Posting and rehearsing emergency procedures	Providing room and space to cool down	Thoughtfully preparing lessons
Preventing bullying and harassment	Demonstrating the process of caring for a plant or class pet	Designing standards-aligned lessons
Reporting classroom concerns around strange odors or signs of mold	Supporting curiosity	Using student data to continuously shape and plan highly differentiated instruction and assessment
Reporting broken or damaged door and window locks and desks	Asking questions about their personal life, weekends, or after-school activities	Participating in professional learning to expand a toolkit of engaging instructional strategies
Ensuring the classroom temperature is comfortable	Checking in with students who have suffered a tragedy or physical illness (loss of family member, accident, serious illness)	Providing consistent progress monitoring reports so students and families can track and advocate for their own learning outcomes

These examples remind us that caring for our students involves assessing physical, mental, and academic needs. It is not just about feeding the hungry, dressing the cold, or hugging the hurting. It is considering how students feel in the school and classroom and adapting the environment to make them feel welcomed. It is also about caring enough to keep them and their parents and guardians informed about how and what they are learning. Care in our classrooms embraces many areas, and the more we allow ourselves to tend to these areas of need, the more we will build trusting relationships that keep us safe.

Think and Write

Using this chart, take some time to engage in a self-assessment around your typical classroom- or school-based acts of care. Using the sample chart provided, reflect on ways you exhibit care for student physical, social-emotional, and academic needs. Write down as many examples as you can think of even if they are sporadic behaviors. While this may take a little time, we firmly believe it is important for each of us to acknowledge how and to what extent we are exhibiting and fostering care, as it is a critical marker of safe learning environments.

Physically	Emotionally	Academically

Challenges to Care

Asking teachers to care as a premise of teaching is not an easily measurable task and is not measured on most teaching evaluations, except in unique assessed categories that include vague notions around engagement with student well-being.

However, as we have already argued, care is the core of every safe and secure classroom. Consider what educational philosopher Nel Noddings noted in her 2005 book *The Challenge to Care in Schools* about the inability for teachers to have the time and resources to truly care for their students:

> It is not surprising that the single greatest complaint of students in these schools is "They don't care!" (Comer, 1988). They feel alienated from their schoolwork, separated from the adults who try to teach them and adrift in a world perceived as baffling and hostile. At the same time, most teachers work very hard and express deep concerns for their students. In an important sense, teachers do care, but are unable to make the connections that would complete caring relations for their students.
>
> (p. 2)

Noddings' spotlight on the gap between wanting to care and actually building a strong, trusting relationship that reflects care hits at the core of what we believe is the greatest challenge we face in today's classrooms. We want to care, we try to care, and we want to respect our learners, but the classroom conditions and school expectations around teaching, leading, and learning have become so overwhelming, and there seems to be no recourse for disruptive behaviors, that making connections is the last thing for which we have time. Why? Because we are just trying to survive—physically, emotionally, and professionally.

As experienced educators, we know firsthand the agony that a teacher feels when she/he wants deeply to care about someone or something but is honestly too fatigued, stressed, or overwhelmed to be able to care, and we believe that many of you reading this book are there now. You are too chronically stressed and fatigued to find an ounce of care, either for yourself or others, at this moment. And if that is where you are, please reach out to us so we can first celebrate you; encourage you; and be a compassionate, listening ear (our contact information is in the back of the book).

Care is challenging at times, often because of core barriers in today's schools. Consider these common barriers to establishing the type of trusting, caring relationships we envision are needed for truly safe schools:

1. **Outside interference:** When outsiders—those who do not know or understand our students or our teaching processes—criticize and hinder efforts to care, life becomes difficult. This might include demands from parents, student advocates, or administrators to change what we know to be the best practices of our content area, to behave differently than we wish to, or to change our classroom expectations or practices. It could also mean applying rules unevenly or even ignoring rules altogether. When outsiders attempt to dictate what is going on in our classrooms, we must be willing to demonstrate, with specific examples and rationale, why our practices, based in care and caring, are justifiable.

2. **Personal problems:** We are humans, and as such, we have our own problems and trials in life. Death, illness, depression, anxiety, family problems, marital difficulties, and even our own personal health issues can weigh on us as we try to care for ourselves and our students. Teachers should not forget it is important to recognize when a personal problem interferes with their ability to care for students. This might come in the form of forgetfulness, loss of ambition, overlooking obvious student emotional concerns, or simply not attempting to resolve problems when they occur. It is not heroic to overlook your own well-being to care for others—in fact, it is more destructive to you in the long run.

3. **Professional turmoil:** When the school building's culture and climate are strained, with colleagues pitted against each other or administrators governing with a heavy hand, your professional life might be at stake. This can occur simultaneously with the idea that it is time to quit the profession. Whether it is a disagreement with parents; a new, unpopular initiative from the school board;

or simply a lack of respect from students, having your professionalism questioned or threatened reduces your capacity to provide a caring classroom for your students.

4. **Behavioral challenges:** Classroom issues, including disruptive and unexplained student behaviors, can interfere with your purpose of setting up a caring learning environment. It can also take an incredible professional toll on our minds and bodies, as behaviors that seem antisocial or disruptive feel personal—as if the student is acting in this way to make life hard for us. When that is how we feel, of course, it is hard to care. It is easier to not care.

The challenges of daily school life and rigors associated with understanding and adapting to student needs can really wear us down and transition care to total apathy. It is the only survival step we have sometimes—to protect our heart, soul, mind, and body, we have to live in a place of apathy, or we might just lose what little sanity we have left. But we all recognize that this is not an enjoyable way to live, so as we think about care, please make sure that self-care is also part of your caring routines. Yes, we want you to teach well, but when that comes at the risk of no time to slow down or rest, then teaching well frankly is not worth it. A classroom cannot exist if you are not there to provide leadership, so take care of you. And with this challenge, we turn to our final thought in this chapter—caring for ourselves and our peers in a positive manner.

The Case for Caring for Our Teachers

We cannot properly address the construct of "care" in our schools without acknowledging how the global pandemic of COVID-19 put teacher care on the front pages of newspapers around the globe. The pandemic, which forced many schools to close, classrooms to shift to online instruction, and teachers to teach math equations from their bathroom showers (because white board markers work well on shower walls), gave us a real-world example of the necessity of teacher care taken to a beautiful extreme.

When the pandemic first hit US schools in the spring of 2020 and state mandates forced many schools to physically close, we witnessed educators caring for students in new and novel ways—from hosting virtual classroom read-alouds at nighttime to help kids fall asleep to sending students handwritten notes saying how much they were missed. Teachers never stopped teaching. They almost immediately shifted and learned how to teach in new and innovative ways. They were checking in on students and their families, working late hours to design new lessons, all while ensuring their own families were cared for as well.

School personnel worked on food distribution and mobile medical care lines, while some special education teachers met special needs students in empty retail store parking lots to provide tactile learning experiences. The nation saw educators take care to an entirely new level, and it was heartwarming, compassionate, and noteworthy.

In this new era, teachers, counselors, principals, and many others became immediate social workers, leaders, technology experts, counselors, providers, facilitators, coaches, and much, much more. They not only cared for students but also fed, clothed, listened to, provided Internet hotspots on school buses, and worked as diligently as they knew how to erase community inequities to level the playing field for all learners in the new normal of schooling.

One of the common themes that soon emerged on social media after everyone realized we were to be in a virtual school model for a while was the level of concern among educators about the safety and security of students at home.

One teacher asked:

But what about all of our students who are not in homes all day where they are not fed, loved, or cared for? What if they are abused? What if nobody in their life right now tells them that they matter?

(Rhea, ninth grade English teacher)

In typical teacher (and leader) fashion, educators worried more about their students than much else as they recognized that for students who were in violent, abusive, or neglectful homes or communities, school was the only safe place to be. This haven had been suddenly removed. Also, for food-deficient families, school was the only place many students got hot meals, and this food source was suddenly cut off (at least temporarily). Educators were scared for their students.

The way that educators cared for kids during this time is perhaps one of the most beautiful stories that came out of a time of deep global crisis, and it just goes to show us that it's very difficult to make educators not care about those they serve. But the hardship of teaching, leading, and learning unfortunately can lead to a place of apathy because once we have exhausted all of our personal compassion, there is little left for self-care.

Why We Care

Asking why we must care about our students and other school community members at this point sounds like a silly question, as we have perhaps already established the idea that care builds trust, which in turn improves safety. But is it in our teaching contract to care? And why should we care for students when they kick us, spit on us, yell "F_ _ k you!," scream in the middle of class, beat up another student in front of us, hit our faces during school fights, and so much more? We have already established that care is hard and almost impossible at times, and we frankly are not paid enough to care sometimes. As previously noted, you are not asked to care for being treated abusively, and you have every right to speak up for conditions that are impossible and that put your safety and security at risk. But being the fine professionals you are, we know you will likely continue to care for students who pose the most risk and challenge, largely because of this question: If we do not care, who will?

I (Lori) recently visited with a former student, now an adult, who grew up in a community of extreme poverty and hardship (with great trauma in the home that included drug use, abandonment, and food instability). After a while, she looked me in the face and said: "Ms. Brown, you are the only person in my life who has ever cared about me." (Sigh . . . sob.)

After I stopped crying and picked myself up off the floor, I hugged her tightly and said, "I do care. I have always cared. You matter. Your life matters. Your happiness matters to me." As we parted ways, I kept crying in my car, but this time they were tears of anger rather than surprise and humility. I was angry that nobody but a teacher had bothered to care for this vulnerable young student and angered that no matter how much I cared, bought her things, and loved her, I could not reverse the trajectory of her life.

Care is hard. But because we are often the one of the only persons caring for our students (or at least in a way that makes a substantial difference), we just cannot ignore the difficulty of it and claim we do not care. Establishing with each student that their life, their thoughts, their ideas, and their challenges have value is one of the most effective steps we can and must do to help our schools establish themselves as communities of care that embrace the best safe and secure school practices.

Wrapping It Up: Students who think, "They really care about me at school" are students who will trust you at times of risk of harm. They will turn to you rather than away from you. The same is true of teachers and leaders. Teachers who think, "My administration or my district really cares about me" will rapidly and willingly work to support administrative practices, protocols, and policies designed to keep everyone safer and more secure.

Never forget—if we do nothing else this school year, we must continuously make it clear that if we are not given the proper resources, time, and abilities to care for our students, for one another, and for ourselves, we are failing every safe school drill that exists. Rules, regulations, drills, and perpetrator deterrents will ultimately do very little to keep us all safe and secure if we are not encouraged and allowed to develop firm, clear, and caring relationships with stakeholders that lead to trusting and collaborative interactions. Remember to challenge your peers and schools to establish safe and secure school policies and procedures that initially stem from solid foundations of caring and compassionate relationships but not abusive or toxic relationships. Only then can safe school practices thrive.

Take Action! Ways Teachers Can Take Action to Build a Caring Classroom

1. Quantify the ways you invest in your classroom— share how much you spend out of pocket on extra supplies or materials with your school leader. Engage with school leaders about realistic budget expenditures and where teachers can provide input into other processes.

2. Champion strategies that allow for longer class periods or smaller class sizes. Volunteer to help school leaders creatively generate options that might change the nature of the traditional schedule in your school.

3. Use language of care when talking about students in conversation. Think carefully before complaining about specific students, pointing out non-academic deficiencies, or making assumptions about student families. Prepare messaging to parents, colleagues, and school leaders that demonstrates your care.

4. Expose the reality that students' learning is directly tied to relationships with teachers to anyone who will listen. Identify specific ways teachers in your school build relationships and community coherently when working with school leaders.

5. Design and teach professional development sessions for your school (and beyond) that specifically address how to care for students.

Reflective Questions for Teachers and Leaders

1. In what ways do your colleagues care for students differently than you?
2. In what ways do you get to know your students or build relationships with them?
3. How do you gather feedback from students about your classroom atmosphere or your relationships? What opportunities do students have to share without fear of retribution?
4. Do you regularly feel as if you care too much, at the detriment of your own well-being? If so, how are you working to find balance?
5. In what ways has caring impacted achievement in your classroom?

6

Valuing Student Voices

I teach students with significant physical challenges. Finn is one of my fourth grad-
ers with limited speech and physical abilities who got left behind during a fire drill
last year. A teaching assistant wheeled him down to the music classroom, expecting the teacher to wheel him inside when the bell rang (this is what she did every
Wednesday). But a fire alarm unexpectedly went off after my assistant stepped
away, the music class evacuated out a side door, and nobody realized Finn was still
sitting in his wheelchair in the main hallway. Thankfully, it was a false alarm. We
realized the mistake quickly and ran back inside and got him out safely, but what if
this had been a real fire and he had been trapped, injured, or even died?

—Hank, elementary special education teacher

How often do you listen to your students? Correction. Adjust
this question so it drives to the real point: How often do you
"hear" your students in a way that promotes stronger, safer, and
more secure relationships and conditions? The need to establish
classrooms of care, built on foundations of cooperative, trusting relationships with clear expectations and outcomes, while
emphasizing the value of your voice in all of these matters is
foundational to classroom management. In this chapter, we begin
the transition to the student voice and to really hearing what may
or may not be verbalized.

We consider the importance of hearing and valuing all student voices (including the voices that make us uncomfortable or
uneasy or that sound very different from the voices we grew up
with), so that everyone has the optimal potential to be kept safe
and secure. After all, safe and secure schools are as much about
the student voice as they are the teacher or leader voice.

DOI: 10.4324/b23214-7

We acknowledge that Finn's story, as tragic as it was, is far from common. We don't believe this happens on a daily basis in schools across America, but Finn's story is a good reminder that if we do not listen to the voices of every stakeholder, including those who cannot physically speak for or remove themselves from dangerous conditions, we may create more chaos than clarity in matters of safe and secure schools.

Consider that Finn is one of many students who potentially cannot advocate for his own safe and secure school needs. Students with physical or emotional challenges that prevent them from easily or rapidly speaking, running, lifting, or moving a wheelchair or leg brace may require expanded assistance in times of routine safe school drills and warnings. In similar fashion, a student whose challenges result in delayed speech patterns may be unable to voice an immediate concern or threat, including the fact that they are choking or feel faint. A student who is on the autism spectrum may struggle with social skills in a way that makes a mandatory class exodus or evacuation with close, herd-like movement near impossible. Finally, consider a hearing-impaired student who is in the restroom when the fire alarm goes off and does not realize the need to evacuate. This student is suddenly placed at a higher level of threat than other students because of the lack of real-time messaging.

We thought it was important to include Finn's story in this text for one simple reason: Safe school conversations mandate we recognize when we are failing to hear and recognize the diverse voices in our schools—including voices that need a little extra layer of care and attention or voices that require technology for sound. If we are not gathering input from everybody, then we are potentially missing risk factors that we have not thought about, and that is not a good thing—especially when it includes you.

If you recall, in prior chapters, we argued that your voice is necessary in conversations about safe and secure schools and that your voice must be loud when conditions or current realities put your health and safety at risk. Well, the same is true for the student who cannot be heard, potentially because of language barriers or physical or mental disabilities that impact communication strategies. Your students need to be heard as often as you want to be heard and valued, so consider how we incorporate their voice in all things about safe and secure schools.

Consider the following students who may feel as if their voices are not heard:

- ◆ A transgender student who is assaulted in the bathroom every other day by peers
- ◆ An overweight student who does not fit under his desk when mandated to go into hiding for an active shooter drill
- ◆ A teacher who is asked to participate in an active shooter drill involving real gunshot sounds, and experiences posttraumatic stress disorder from a prior life experience at the age of 16 in which he/she witnessed a drive by community shooting leading to a neighbor's death
- ◆ A student who is petrified to share with school staff that she is receiving cyber threats from an older male stalker through her school-based email account
- ◆ An 11th grade gay couple that wants to attend prom together but has received threatening texts stating that showing up together at prom means they will never make it home

In each case, you find students who may have the physical and cognitive abilities to speak up and speak out to promote safer or more secure learning environments, but they may be choosing to remain silent for personal reasons—reasons that, to them, ensure their safety. Choosing to remain silent is not in the best interest of the school or district, so we must find ways to encourage students to talk, to report, and to find a trusted adult when one is needed. Students may choose to hide in their silence, but we can do everything we can to create a safe reporting structure in which the possibility of shared safety is more appealing than the isolation of supposed safety.

Questions for the Reader

Have you dealt with a student who obviously felt some measure of fear but refused to explain what was happening out of fear that something might happen if they spoke up? If so, how did you handle this challenge?

While we know firsthand that our schools do an incredible job of working to give opportunity to each student's voice, the reality is that many students in our buildings still fail to be heard. Many school districts have launched anonymous reporting tip lines or websites where students (or anyone) can report rumors or concerns about school safety. These reporting mechanisms have encouraged some students to share perceived threats and questionable behaviors without fear of retribution. In fact, having an anonymous reporting tip line is considered a best practice in safe and secure schools. But still, far too many tips go unreported because students are alarmed about being labeled as someone who cannot keep quiet.

Student peer culture is often about perception, with frequent attempts to appear mature and capable beyond one's own age or true capabilities. It is very easy to get wrapped up in youthful culture and to forget that someone who is flashing a gun may actually want to do more with that gun than show and tell.

But social acceptance of the flashy weapon can result in horrendous consequences, as the failure to speak out about potential threats has deep ripple effects in communities and schools. Consider the two Ohio juveniles charged with failure to report that a classmate had a gun on campus (Pack, 2016). Silenced voices are rarely a good thing for anybody involved, and as we see in Ohio, silenced voices (whether by choice or pressure) lead to legal crises, as persons may be formally charged with failure to report something that could have prevented an act of violence.

The same is true of teachers and school staff. Being an adult and a working professional does not remove one from threats or questionable behaviors by colleagues. The professional community that we establish in each of our schools and districts provides an opportunity to face multiple fears. Like our students, we may choose to stay silent for reasons that are not limited to but may include being perceived as a nosy teacher, being ostracized from our peers, misunderstanding someone's intent and getting them in trouble with the administration for nothing, or a myriad of other reasons that can hinder our professional standing among our peers.

Sometimes we, like our students, fail to speak up and let our voices be heard in matters of safe and secure schools out of concern for how we will be perceived in the larger community. If our peers believe we are simply informants for school leaders, we will find ourselves isolated. But when fear of or the failure to speak up overrides saying something about a potential threat, then we put others at risk. For this reason, we need to discuss the importance of modeling and encouraging our students to raise their voices regularly.

What Would You Do?

Mr. Bisset teaches ninth grade physical education classes and coaches varsity soccer. Consequently, he has key access to the gym and other key athletic locations on campus. One of his male colleagues, Ray Connor, occasionally uses the gym weight room as well. One day Mr. Bisset has his third block students using the gym equipment when an unfortunate accident occurs. A weight slips off its bar and falls on a student's foot, breaking a toe. Mr. Bisset knows why this happened. His colleague, Ray, failed to properly secure the equipment the night before when in use. Now put yourself in Mr. Bisset's shoes. What do you do? You knew Ray was getting lazy with the upkeep of the weights because he always claimed how tired and busy he was, but speaking up will potentially get him suspended from his job and will destroy a friendship and professional working relationship. Do you speak up, considering one of your students has now required hospital emergency attention and the parents are furious?

As we place ourselves into Mr. Bisset's situation, we suddenly realize why our students are scared or hesitant to speak up and speak out about students who carry a gun to school, who have illegal substances in their backpacks, or who have made threats against the school on social media platforms. Saying something may mean we find ourselves unliked and alone. But silence really isn't an option when the care of others is at stake. For this reason, consider how we embrace all student voices and establish the right environment for full transparency and acceptance among diverse and valuable student, staff, and stakeholder voices.

The Importance of Student Voice

Student voices host the heartbeat of the school. Student voices tell us whether students feel valued, secure, and cared for and whether they are getting the message that learning is a priority. In a sobering way, student voices also tell us whether students believe they would be missed if they were gone. In this way, their voices can be the catalyst to positive change.

Student voice is additionally critical to building the caring community relationships that we said mattered in prior chapters. If you think about how you personally build dating, marriage, or familial relationships, then you will understand and be able to promote the idea that building relationships requires strong verbal and non-verbal communication skills. A relationship is a two-way communication pathway, one in which being heard and having the ability to share have equal value.

Without rigorous, robust, caring, and compassionate dialogue with others (either personally or professionally), how are we to understand the fears, tears, joys, and celebrations of those we study with, work alongside, or spend our days with? If we want to hear student voices well, then our first step has to be engagement. You will never truly hear a voice if you are not directly engaged with that voice in meaningful dialogue. Be purposeful in how you engage with students for safer and more secure schools.

But pause for a moment and dig a bit deeper into this mandate to engage in purposeful student conversation. When we choose to engage in purposeful dialogue with students, how are we to respond when the things they tell us are horrible, disturbing, violent, or illegal? What are we to do with student voices that leave us scared or fill us with such horrific stories of abuse, neglect, or violence that we are frozen into a state of inaction? And what do we do with the student voice that is simply too invasive—one that crosses the line between teacher and student?

Are we meant to say, "Oops; sorry I asked! Forget we talked?" Or should we respond meaningfully and take action specific to the topics or themes that frighten us? Seeking to hear student voices comes at a cost, for sure, and we need to be ready to respond to the sobering reality of "real talk" because students enjoy using their voices and find multiple purposes to raise them loudly.

Ways Students Use Their Voices

If you have ever supervised lunch duty in a school cafeteria or supervised a middle school field trip on big yellow buses, then you know student voices can be loud, chaotic, and overwhelming.

But student voices do not always come in the form of loud, obnoxious, or annoying cafeteria screams and squabbles. In fact, student voices sometimes make no physical sound at all.

Consider the connectivity, accessibility, and frequency of student communications in today's technologically-connected society. Students need not utter a physical word to engage in extensive conversation and dialogue on the computer or on their cell phone. They can send messages that disappear within hours or that live forever on the Internet.

As students have become more connected to each other, their means of spreading messages, gossip, rumors, and thoughts about school and the lives they live in a local community have taken many different forms:

- Speeches and letters
- Newspapers
- Texts, blogs, notes, and letters to the editor
- Facebook messages
- Snapchat
- TikTok videos
- Instagram images
- Email and tip lines
- Journals
- Assignments
- Novels
- T-shirts slogans, artwork, and poems
- Hallway chatter
- Assemblies and protests

Some students use their voices to express opinions, protest, or merely engage socially with their classmates. At times, we hear these voices, and we cringe, asking ourselves, "Why did they just do that or say that?" But other times, student voices are deeply meaningful and purposeful for matters of school safety. Consider the positive ways student voices can be used as an expression of their larger purposes and power within a collaborative, engaged, and caring school community:

- Provide feedback on processes and policies.
- Offer preferences on learning activities or selected content.
- Provide a verbal or written assessment of the equity within curriculum.
- Share safety concerns, including rumors or speculation heard in the hallways in writing, to support or criticize school leaders or teachers.

- ◆ Bring about change around the way students are treated by school staff.
- ◆ Spark debate about difficult issues close to the hearts of the student population.
- ◆ Plan future events or directions for the school.
- ◆ Rally around a teacher with cancer.
- ◆ Promote community connections and volunteer to help in times of need.
- ◆ Instigate a process addressing the well-being of fellow students.

Within five weeks of the 2018 Parkland, Florida, shooting at Marjory Stoneman Douglas High School, students from Parkland (and all over the nation) organized the "March for Our Lives," a nationwide gun control event. CNN reported the five steps the students took to organize the event quickly: first, they took immediate action within days of the shooting. They engaged with the media, raised needed funds, built momentum from small legislative victories, and welcomed support from others (Grinberg & Muaddi, 2018).

The speed with which students mobilized their grief and horror into advocacy and action is impressive, and it reminds us that student voices can be powerful forces for change, including in matters of safe and secure schools. With this movement, we saw student voice as a positive expression when it forces us to become more inclusive of diverse strategies, approaches, and goals around how we choose to do school life together and protect that life.

We may get frustrated by students who choose to use their voices for disruption and dissent, particularly when it pulls them out of the classroom and we lose valuable teaching time, but at the end of the day, our students, and in fact, all students, have a right to be heard, ethically, morally, and legally, at school, much like you have a right to be heard and valued. Allowing even dissenting voices is critical when we seek to build a safe and secure environment. As stated earlier, silenced voices lead us to less stable environments because too many people fear speaking up and speaking out about matters that could control pending acts of harm or violence.

Now, return to the student voice that is not engaged in a protest or purpose but still impacts our daily school life in a way that makes us uncomfortable.

Student Voices That Surprise and Shock Us

Students say things, do things, and hear things that shock us, disarm us, and make us question if what they say is actually based in reality. We (Lori and Gretchen) brainstormed some of the funny and not-so-funny moments from our classroom teaching time—times when students looked us in the eye or blurted out random remarks during class. We think you will get a laugh out of our real-world examples:

- ◆ Your shoes don't match. One is blue, and one is black!
- ◆ Did you know that when the light hits your skirt, you can see through it?
- ◆ What did you do to your hair? It's weird today.
- ◆ Why don't you wear earrings?
- ◆ Why don't you have a girlfriend/boyfriend?
- ◆ You don't look good today.
- ◆ Why are you in such a bad mood?
- ◆ What did you eat for lunch?
- ◆ This is just stupid.
- ◆ I don't know why you bother to teach. You don't know what you're talking about.
- ◆ My dad can explain this crap to me better than you can.
- ◆ Why did you make us do that f_ _ king assignment? It was just busy work because you can't teach.

Unfortunately, and perhaps without purposeful intent, student voices that say these things can be harsh and too invasive even when they do not realize that is the case. There is, after all, a brutal honesty that accompanies teaching that can be simultaneously refreshing and startling. But as annoying or frustrating as such random or hurtful remarks can be, they do not come close to making the kind of impact that violent voices make on our hearts and minds.

When Student Voice Becomes Violent, Dark, or Disturbing

Students, at times, say things that are rude, demeaning, illogical, childish, or annoying, as acknowledged in the previous section. And it is particularly worse when students voice a thought for no reason other than to be purposefully disruptive, and as teachers, we should not be okay with the purposefully disruptive voice. But sometimes student voices, particularly when students write their thoughts down on paper, signal that we have a student in crisis.

Consider the following real-world examples of violent or dark themes teachers have received from students in writing and immediately questioned whether they or the other students were at risk of harm:

- ◆ A high school student tasked with writing about his future explained how he wanted to assume a dictatorial leadership role like his personal idol, Adolf Hitler, watching people fall at his feet.
- ◆ A fifth grade student wrote a Halloween story that was so dark and filled with excessive references to murders and amputations that the teacher called for a parent conference immediately after reading the text.
- ◆ A middle school student who was tasked about writing about heroes wrote about Klebold and Harris, the Columbine High School mass shooters.
- ◆ A ninth grade student turned in a creative writing piece about a teenager who was gang raped, assaulted, and slapped around by a group of drunken college boys. The description of the imaginary character all but fit the physical description of the student who wrote the text.
- ◆ A sixth grade student composed a school journal entry about cutting her own arms and described in detail how

the blood fell in the bathtub as she cut deeper and deeper, releasing the pain of her parents' divorce.

♦ An 11th grade student tasked with writing a letter to his English teacher (and that teacher happened to be author Gretchen Oltman) wrote the following: "I am the worst person you'll ever meet. I like to pa-a-a-a-rty and shoot guns. I would watch out if I were you" (Oltman, 2012, p. xx)

♦ A senior in high school showed her classmate a poem at lunch in which she wrote: "I'm a mean bitch and school is what I ditch. Don't make me learn, or my gun will make a turn. You better watch your back, 'cause it may end up in a body sack."

The information we learn from our students' written words raise significant red flags that real harm or ill will is possible, plausible, and ready to erupt. If we stop to consider that many of our nation's known school shooters prefaced their dark and deadly deeds with school-based assignments referencing themes of murder, death, or disturbing historical figures, we might conclude that references to anything dark mean someone wants to engage in dark and deadly behaviors. Here are just a few examples showing that it has happened:

♦ Kip Kinkel, Thurston High School shooter in 1998, wrote a school essay about love in which he indicated that only firearms could help him fight his unloved "cold, black heart" (Lieberman, 2008, p. 95).

♦ Nicholas Cruz, Marjory Stoneman Douglas High School shooter, posted on Instagram that he wanted to shoot up the school a full two years before he actually committed the mass shooting (Rose, 2018).

♦ Barry Loukaitis, Frontier Junior High School shooter in 1996, wrote ninth grade poems that carried a violent theme. One poem was titled "Murder" (Fast, 2009, p. 33).

Student expressions of violence (in writing or shared in conversations with others) prior to the commission of violent acts are not rare, as violent perpetrators are known to leak their intentions prior to violent acts. For this reason, dark, disturbing, or simply uncomfortable student words must not be ignored. We must remain vigilant and attentive when we see themes that make us stop and wonder if the student is facing a crisis.

While even the FBI agrees that most students who write of dark and violent themes are doing nothing more than exercising creative liberty with their assigned tasks, there are those who write of such themes as they plan and prepare for dark and deadly deeds—and we must be vigilant to be attentive to this when it shows up on our desks (O'Toole, 1999).

Paying attention to questionable student themes that may alert us that something is not quite right provides the foundation for potentially engaging local law enforcement or mental health partners. Patterns of student produced themes or topics that border on inappropriate or threatening should come before those who have the skill set to determine if there is a real-world threat, but we urge you to exercise caution in this process. Our best approach is a balanced approach to student voices—both verbal or written voices—that give us significant pause. We find balance by following a few key principles, including:

♦ Violent voices are valuable voices. They should not be silenced.
♦ Student voice is an expression of self-worth and value. Allow all voices to be heard.
♦ Find the positive in voices that disturb. View these voices as an opportunity to potentially help a student get the help or support they need to find a better place of personal balance.
♦ Let the voices of your colleagues help you make wise decisions about student voice.

Truly violent and threatening student expression is not protected by any Constitutional or legal principle. That is, a student who threatens to shoot a teacher, set a bomb off in a school, or attack another student has no legal standing to do so and should be immediately reported to school leaders and law enforcement officials. The issue, though, is that as educators, we are not trained to know when a remark is creative expression, humor, or a real threat, and that is why schools must rely on community partners and internal school staff trained in this arena.

Remember this—you do not, nor should you ever, tolerate violence or real threats. You need to remain aggressive with school leadership and let your voice be heard, for your own safety and security, along with that of your students.

Friendly Reminder

A teaching license is not a license to put yourself in harm's way, so please remember that there is much a school can do, with community partners, to intervene and help reverse a pattern of behavior that is leading to a dangerous act.

The Importance of Being Heard

We explained that student voice matters, but what is the greater significance of students being heard? Do we promote student voice because it is the most inclusive approach to schooling, or is there something to be said about a student's legal right to expression?

In the United States, precedent from the US Supreme Court reinforces the idea that student voices should not be needlessly silenced. From the armbands worn to protest the Vietnam War in *Tinker v. Des Moines* to the debate about who controls the content of school newspapers in *Hazelwood v. Kuhlmeier*, the need to find ways for students to have a voice within schools is more than just a feel-good effort.

Psychologically, being heard gives significance to your thoughts, feelings, emotions, and values. When students feel heard in schools, they feel invested, important, and essential to school functions. Whether their message is positive or negative, students are the largest group of stakeholders we have in our schools, and we would be wise to at least listen to what they are trying to tell us.

> Students need to be able to express themselves; the freedom to do so is not only a question of their intellectual development but also one of human rights. School kids may well rebel at the rules. They may challenge authority, or, God forbid, even resist. But punishing students for their political beliefs or their opinion of their school is to chastise developmentally appropriate behavior. Believe it or not, students have views on how good (or not) a school is beyond a standardized test score—and it's in our best interest to hear them. They know their schools; plus, education is meant to help students grow, to help them be free-thinking citizens. Alas, many school leaders seem too afraid of what their students are thinking to let them voice those thoughts out loud, and they suppress their students' rights in the process.
>
> (Perry, 2018, para. 1–2)

Being heard is, ironically, a critical part of one's self-image and self-efficacy, as silenced voices often become discouraged voices that doubt their own power and purpose. Additionally, silenced, discouraged voices may stubbornly stay silent when we desperately need them to speak. But as is often the case in education, we have to find balance in all things.

But how do we allow for open voices when the topics they present hold the potential to leave us unsettled, frightened, confused, or ready to quit the profession? Do we still let them talk, or should we immediately censor dialogue in our classrooms? We argue that dialogue should be encouraged, and when a phrase or idea troubles you, you need to act. Your gut will tell you when a student has blurted out something that you recognize is either atypical or sounds truly frightening. Following shortly is a T3 protocol you can use to help with dialogue that turns dangerous.

To foster strong dialogue, you might consider some of these creative avenues (Pandolpho, 2020) for full expression of student voice:

♦ Class meetings
♦ Anonymous tip lines
♦ Surveys
♦ Advisory groups
♦ Collaborative projects
♦ Rituals
♦ Participation in morning announcements
♦ Small focus groups with teachers or school leaders

These suggestions promote the idea that there are many ways to allow voices to sound off and to speak out, in both verbal and nonverbal ways. To honor the unique expression of our students, we must consider embracing facilitated and supportive approaches to hearing what they think, feel, have witnessed, or want. And for optimal school safety and security, an anonymous tip line is not just a good idea but rather a must have. Research shows us that anonymous reporting will lead to more stakeholders reporting potentially threatening behaviors in time for law enforcement to act.

The US Department of Homeland Security maintains a "see something—say something" presence online and across the nation. The idea behind this campaign is that we all keep our nation and local communities safer when we speak up about something we have witnessed that could indicate someone is thinking about doing something dangerous. If this principle is good enough for the nation as a whole, then we should also embrace it in our local schools. Students must believe they can report or offer a tip on a potential threat without fear of retribution if their voices are going to make a full impact on the safety and security of our schools.

Tips for Addressing Uncomfortable Voices in the Classroom

Our T3 protocol has been designed to provide you with an approach to responding to the student voices that become annoying, intrusive, overwhelming, or potentially threatening. We want you to have a good starting place so you respond as comprehensively as possible to help your larger school community help you. Consider the following protocol:

Teacher Tools: T3 Assessment Protocol

Step 1: Temper

First, temper your internal fears and acknowledge that violent or disturbing student expression is usually innocuous. Consider the environment in which kids are raised today—even movies and television shows for young children can host a variety of violent content. The violent expression may emerge from a movie or book they absorbed the week before. Or it may be an expression of violence they have witnessed in the local community. Writing through lived trauma is a common response for victims, so it should not surprise us when students write of such themes. It may also be the only way a student feels safe in sharing witnessed or experienced trauma. As you temper fears and emotions, remember that you have a relationship with this student, and that gives you the opportunity to dig a little deeper and ask exploratory questions. In short, do not assume that violent expressions mean someone wants to act violently unless it is a direct threat (e.g., "I want to bring a bomb to school and blow up mean people").

Step 2: Talk

Next, sit down and talk with the student in a one-on-one setting. Approach the conversation without fear and be willing to listen carefully. Ask questions about what they wrote and why they wrote it. What was going through their head at the time? A good way to initiate the conversation is as follows: "I'd like to chat with you about this essay, drawing, etc. It contained some violent, graphic descriptions. I haven't seen this sort of writing from you before. Help me understand why you chose these themes." In many cases, students will openly share their motivations behind the piece, which clarifies intent. But if they indicate that the disturbing text is indicative of thoughts they've had (e.g., I hate myself, and I've thought of suicide) or they try to evade the questions and act strangely about the text, then elevate the concern to school based mental health staff (see step 3 next). If you truly feel threatened by the student (i.e., the student has a history of violence against others, has threatened you or others before, or has made a viable threat to your safety), it may be necessary to contact your school-based administrators or law enforcement in lieu of meeting individually with the student.

Step 3: Take Action

Finally, take action. Your action may be to drop the concern after a thorough student conversation. But in some cases, your gut tells you that you need to do something more. This is especially the case when you have noticed a pattern of violent expressions from this student over time or you have witnessed a radical personality change. Always consider taking a higher level of action if the student conversation leaves you dissatisfied and unsettled. Options include (1) talking to the student's other teachers to see if they have witnessed similar themes, (2) asking the school-based mental health staff to get engaged, (3) talking with a school administrator to see if they've had any concerns about the student's prior behaviors or choices, (4) talking with the student's parents, or (5) turning the text or drawing over to a school-based threat assessment team (this choice should always involve school administration).

Remember that teachers are not trained threat assessors or psychologists, meaning alarming or concerning expressions should be referred to those who are trained to properly address them. Please remember that direct threats should always be handled immediately and with swift response from the administration, local law enforcement, and a threat assessment team.

Take Action! Ways Teachers Can Bring Attention to Student Voice

1. Add student membership to school committees whenever possible, including hiring, policy, and disciplinary committees.
2. Teach students appropriate and legal ways to protest, including ways change has been accomplished throughout history through speaking up, peacefully protesting, and becoming involved in community change.
3. Sponsor student clubs and activities that prepare students to be active and informed citizens.
4. Tell the stories of your students to policymakers and school leaders.
5. Provide opportunities and feedback for students to practice writing and speaking in public forums.

Reflective Questions for Teachers and Leaders

1. In this chapter, we considered the student voice as a voice or purpose, power, and protest. Would you add anything else to these descriptors?
2. What conditions or circumstances lead you to want to silence student voices and why?
3. Have you ever worked in a school that actively embraced student voice with committees or critical school decisions about various topics—from curriculum and instruction to safety and security? If you have not, what do you think about this role for student voices?
4. If you could identify and solidify a larger place or role for the student voice in your building, what might that look like and feel like?

5. Have you ever received a disturbing student voice that left you so rattled or shaken you took steps to respond, either by engaging other staff or with the student's parents? Share what happened and how you chose to respond.

7

Trauma

I was a student in high school when the Columbine High School shootings happened. I remember watching that tragedy on TV and then forming the idea in my head that we are not safe in school. Then the attacks on September 11, 2001, took place during my freshman year of college. Again, more fear and the belief that we really are not safe anywhere. As I grew into adulthood and was living on my own, it became very apparent that we live in a scary world. As an educator, I frequently work with families feeling the same. And you know, I get it because I lived through those life-changing traumatic events. Trauma in the lives of our kids is real.

—Camilla, veteran elementary special education teacher

Trauma is a popular topic in today's schools. From conference sessions and professional learning workshops to publisher-promoted books and trauma-informed networks, educators have multiple opportunities to study the concept of trauma and its impact on students and stakeholders and to better understand the ripple effect trauma can have on teaching, leading, and learning conditions—and for good reason.

Today's students arrive at school with lived experiences (from poverty to neglect and from abuse to illiteracy) that significantly impede or interfere with learning. We would be negligent to ignore that trauma is not a reality for our students and teachers, particularly for those who lived through the COVID-19 global pandemic.

In 2017, the children's television show *Sesame Street* introduced new programming that included explicit strategies to teach kids how to cope with trauma (Chandler, 2017). When the impact of trauma on our youngest learners becomes significant

DOI: 10.4324/b23214-8

enough for thematic development in children's television programming, then it is perhaps past the time to ask how and why trauma impacts our teaching, leading, and learning processes.

Prior to the global pandemic, many trauma-related conversations in schools centered on students who have been significantly impacted by conditions of poverty, neglect, abuse, community violence, or from extreme rare events (mass shootings, tornados, fires, and floods). COVID-19 significantly expanded trauma-based conversations to include themes of isolation and secondary trauma.

Many wondered how students who could not attend school, engage with peers, or receive hot meals and weekly care by school staff would survive in homes filled with chaos and crisis? How would educators who felt traumatized by their students' trauma (e.g., secondary trauma) respond and react during this strange season of life? And where would all of this lead us in the long run?

Trauma in the lives of our students can force us to see, hear, and witness things that we cannot understand. It is particularly agonizing when we see a once vibrant student go silent or act in ways that present a major disruption to the learning environment. Because teachers build relationships with those they teach, we know when something has changed or when personalities shift in significant ways.

Because trauma can lead to a ripple effect of anti-social or unexplainable behaviors that hold the potential, at times, to lead to expanded aggressive or dangerous behaviors, we must now turn our attention to all things "trauma related" if we are to maintain safe and secure schools. The emotional and behavioral responses that can emerge from unaddressed trauma in the life of a student or stakeholder can be a threat to our efforts to build and maintain a safe and secure school.

Questions for the Reader

In recent years, have you been asked to participate in a trauma-focused professional learning session? If so, how did it shape your daily practice? What trauma-informed strategies do you utilize in your teaching?

As we think about the impact trauma can have on our schools, we want you to place priority on reflecting about your own knowledge or training around how to address students who are exhibiting signs that they may be traumatized. We also want to ask you to enter this topic of trauma by considering how your students' trauma may have already impacted you (secondary trauma). Finally, how have traumatizing experiences you have personally faced shaped your career as an educator? Keep these questions in mind as reflect on trauma in today's schools. To get us started, consider what we mean by the construct and look at the numbers that shape our classrooms.

Trauma Defined

Trauma is an emotional response to a terrible event like an accident, rape, or natural disaster. (American Psychological Association, 2020, para. 1)

Hard times, difficult experiences, and loss can leave a person traumatized. But trauma impacts persons in unique ways, meaning trauma may look and feel different for even a group of students who have jointly experienced a shocking and disruptive event together (think something like a natural disaster, a car accident, the loss of a friend to cancer, or even a mass shooting).

We tend to think of trauma as an event or explicit time in a student's life when she/he was scared, neglected, or frightened. For example, a student's mother died, a family member was injured, a family lost everything they owned due to a fire and so on. However, trauma can emerge from multiple events over a larger season of time (e.g., years of homelessness, decades of abuse, months of abandonment).

The Centers for Disease Control and Prevention (CDC; n.d., para. 1) describes traumatic events as follows:

Most everyone has been through a stressful event in his or her life. When the event, or series of events, causes a lot of stress, it is called a traumatic event. Traumatic events are marked by a sense of horror, helplessness, serious injury, or the threat of serious injury or death. Traumatic events affect survivors, rescue workers, and the friends and relatives of victims who have been involved. They may also have an impact on people who have seen the event either firsthand or on television.

Trauma based on one life event is challenging enough, but think for just a moment about our students who experience two, three, or four traumatizing events in a short span of time. How do we expect they can function with the impact of repeated pain? Short answer: they cannot.

The idea that our nation's youngest and most vulnerable people are potentially facing multiple traumatic events before they even hit adulthood is of such concern that much attention has been given to the study of what are often called "ACES" or (adverse childhood experiences). Nationally, 1 in every 10 children has experienced three or more ACES. That is way too much trauma before adulthood, meaning we must embrace the fact that our students are coming to us at the age of 5 or 6 years already a bit broken and battered by the lives they have lived (Sacks & Murphey, 2018).

Trauma by the Numbers

Unfortunately, Substance Abuse and Mental Health Services Administration (SAMHSA) (2022) reports that by the age of 16 years, more than two-thirds of our children have experienced at least one traumatic event. This could be anything from psychological or sexual abuse to being witness to domestic violence, experiencing a sudden loss (death), neglect, severe accidents, and much more. Unfortunately, the trends don't get better with age. Trend data reveal that our high school students are also in crisis.

Consider the following about today's high school students:

◆ Each day, more than 1,000 youth visit emergency departments because of physical assaults (CDC, Fast Fact, Preventing Youth, 2021).

- For persons between the ages of 10–24 years, homicide is the third leading cause of death, and this rate increases for African-American and non-Hispanic Black persons (CDC, Fast Fact, Preventing Youth, 2021).
- One of every six teenagers reports being cyberbullied, while one of every five reports facing real-world bullying behaviors on school property (CDC, Preventing Bullying, 2021).

Couple any or all of these experiences with the number of families that have lived through natural disasters (tornados, floods, hurricanes, fires, and other unexpected events), endured city violence (neighborhood-based violence), or faced sudden unemployment leading to the loss of financial stability, and you have a national student body that is distracted by the stress and horrors of life.

Understanding where trauma starts is helpful, but for our daily school practices—safe and secure practices—we need to know more about the **result** of trauma. After all, we are not in our students' lives every hour of every day, so we have to admit that we teach them in the condition in which they arrive in our classroom—and that is a sobering reality that much of the world fails to see when they examine the field of teaching.

Question for the Reader

What can and should we expect if we have a student who has endured a traumatic event or condition but we do not have details about the horror? How might this impact your teaching?

You may never know when a student or stakeholder has lived through a traumatic event. But at times, you will see and experience behaviors that can be as extreme as violent actions, meltdowns, random outbursts, emotional disruptions, disengagement, anger, or a variety of other responses. The key here is that there is no one response to trauma, and as classroom teachers, we must be ready for anything. Thus, we also must prepare ourselves with the tools to secure resources for our students when we recognize a trauma has occurred. We must also agree that professionally, we need training and strategies for recognizing and teaching trauma-impacted students and that our response will not be that it is not our problem.

You see, a safe classroom recognizes the reality of the lived experiences of those who have shown up to learn. Instead of pretending that trauma is beyond our expertise (which, quite honestly, it is beyond our expertise), we need to step up and be advocates for ourselves and our students to get the resources possible, so teaching and learning processes will be smoother.

Behavioral and Bodily Responses to Trauma

In school, children with trauma are more likely to have trouble regulating their emotions, focusing, and interacting with peers and adults in a positive way. (Kris, 2018, para. 3)

As teachers, we may know a lot of "stuff," but we rarely know what truly drives a learner to experience trauma or to what extent a student has experienced trauma, which leaves us guessing, many days, about a student's lived experiences. Sometimes we have no clue that a student has lived through horrors until suddenly the student shares a personal story or bursts out with a scream, cry, or behavior because they have finally had enough and the trauma and emotions inside know of no other way to escape than through a loud, bold, or sometimes violent act.

As psychiatrist Dr. Nancy Rappaport stated about traumatized children, "They are masters at making sure you do *not* see them bleed" (as cited in Miller, 2020, para. 2). Students often do not want to be seen as "different" or "difficult" in school, so even when they need our help or the help of specialized counselors, they are often not going to ask for it. They do not want to stand out or risk of being ridiculed. But trauma left unaddressed will manifest in significant ways.

Characteristics of Traumatized Persons

Trauma comes in a multitude of manners, traits, habits, and indicators. While there is no one clear cause for trauma—in fact, trauma can come from many potential sources and events—many resources directed at teachers today attempt to place the weight of student trauma on teacher shoulders. Potential markers of psychological trauma include: (Cascade Behavioral Health in Washington State, 2022):

- ◆ Loss of memory
- ◆ Lack of concentration skills
- ◆ Anger
- ◆ Mood swings
- ◆ Confusion
- ◆ Lack of interest in previously enjoyed activities
- ◆ Extreme fatigue
- ◆ Anxiety
- ◆ Guilt
- ◆ Shame
- ◆ Detached from emotions
- ◆ Perfectionism
- ◆ Excessive need for other's approval
- ◆ Personality extremes to draw attention to oneself
- ◆ Detached from other people

Trauma or repeated traumatic events impact the mind and body (Hall & Souers, 2016). When a student who has prior trauma faces a triggering event that brings up negative memories, their body often embraces a fight or flight experience (either I fight this or I get away from it so it cannot bother me anymore). When this happens at school and the student feels trapped (flight does not appear possible), then their only option may be fight—to physically respond to the trigger. This is when we see behaviors that may leave us scratching our heads or wondering what we did to evoke this response among our students.

Rappaport identifies how trauma can lead to behaviors that we may see in school settings. The list is not limited to but includes:

♦ **Trouble forming relationships with teachers** or the inability to build trust, ask for help, or simply to be understood by an adult in the classroom. One important note here is that if we acknowledge that one of the main influences on a successful student's educational experience is building meaningful relationships with teachers at school, we already see a dissonance in why traumatized students struggle.

♦ **Poor self-regulation** or the inability to control emotions. This might manifest in outbursts, inappropriate emotional responses, or lack of an appropriate emotional response.

♦ **Negative thinking:** Dr. Rappaport explains that traumatized students "see negative where we see neutral." That is, there is an internal voice telling the student that negative experiences are their fault, they are to blame, and they are not worthy of good things. In the classroom, consider how praise and feedback can be misconstrued by a traumatized student.

♦ **Hypervigilance** or always seeking to protect oneself. Imagine this as a heightened fight-or-flight sense in which the student is acutely aware of small things that may signal danger. Hypervigilance can be exhausting and can lead to behavior issues for many students.

♦ **Executive function challenges:** This might be not being able to follow simple directions, complete a task, or plan for next week's lesson. Students may have a distorted sense of the future—perhaps one of looming disruption and trauma, which makes completing tasks difficult.

Consider these behaviors in a classroom setting, although we acknowledge that many of you see these responses almost daily in today's classroom, so little imagination is needed.

Scenario #1: Imagine a 10th grade student sitting in high school geometry class feeling overwhelmed and shocked about the trauma life has just dealt through the unexpected death of his 18-year-old cousin. This 10th grade student, Jacob, is upset, angry, and disillusioned. How could life take his cousin at such a young age? He was just a few years older than Jacob!

Jacob is trying desperately to process this, and he knows he is distracted, but his geometry teacher keeps selecting him to respond to and solve word problems. As his agitation grows and the teacher calls on his for the third time in an hour, Jacob stands up, yells a profane remark, and walks out of the room. Jacob has chosen to flee this situation (fight or flight—he chose flight).

When an administrator responds to this troubling behavior by assigning after-school truancy or one-day out of school suspension, which is a pretty typical response to a student verbally assaulting a teacher with profanities, we know that nothing will ultimately change inside of Jacob or with his chosen behaviors. Why? Because the suspension does not address the core issue left unresolved—built-up anger, frustration, and disillusionment with life's hardships and loss.

In this particular scenario, no traditional disciplinary action can resolve what is really going on in Jacob's head and heart. Jacob's issue isn't behavior. It is trauma mixed with some grief and layered with sadness. He is disillusioned by life's cruel hand to take someone he loved deeply far too early. Unfortunately, this is one part of the human experience.

Scenario #2—Consider another example—a student who takes apathy to a whole new level. If sixth grader Jason feels hopeless, slighted, and ignored because his first girlfriend dumped him two days ago and screamed he was ugly, then he may believe no one will ever like or love him and that life is just hopeless. His heart has been crushed. So, the last thing on his mind is learning how to paint with acrylic paints in his art elective. Consequently, he sits at the art table, staring at an empty canvas. Will a traditional disciplinary or teacher response work well here? Probably not.

Jason's problem runs much deeper than apathy, as the heart of his pain is loss, frustration, and questions about his self-worth. Now, is Jason's issue really "trauma related?" Probably not. Jason's concern is likely more about traditional middle school trauma and the heartache of losing his first love. It would be hard to say he is traumatized deeply, but if his girlfriend's rejection is just one of many rejections he has faced in the past year (his mother left home, his grandmother died, and more), then there could be a pattern of trauma building in his young life.

The fact that trauma can drive unexplainable behavior is why many teachers advocate for avoiding labeling traumatized students as "bad students." They are not bad. They are instead broken and need a level of help that no in-school or out-of-school suspension can fix.

But accepting this and living with a student in the classroom who disrupts, yells, and exhibits physically and emotionally violent behavior is far easier said than done, as these behaviors often make our jobs all but impossible. While we all know that traditional disciplinary responses to anti-social or potentially dangerous or violent student outburst rarely fixes the problem, we cannot just let a student tear up the classroom, scream at others until his/her face turns another color, and scare everyone in the area. Or can we? In many cases today, it feels like teachers are being told to just overlook these trauma-induced behaviors and instead adopt trauma-informed classroom practices. But we honestly believe that this is not the best response or an easy quick fix. As professional educators, we are deeply troubled about the idea of ignoring intense behaviors and labeling them as trauma induced, because of the ripple effect of what this does to the teachers and other students who experienced the intense event or behavior. It is not good for anyone involved. In our rush to identify every negative, anti-social behavior as trauma related and to push for alternative responses, we have forgotten the teacher who is left behind in the classroom asking, "How does the student who just screamed that I'm a fucking bitch and destroyed everything on my desk get to just sit in the office with no consequences?" And when this question is asked, we are starting down the dangerous slope of losing a really good teacher.

When a school chooses to embrace deeper trauma-informed practiced for purposes of trying to get to the root cause of unexplained, intense student behaviors, it can leave the teacher feeling angry, frustrated, and apathetic because it feels like nothing is being done. And this is something we must tackle if we're going to talk seriously about trauma-informed strategies. Your authors are not against trauma-informed practices or responses, but we do want to see balance in all things. Consider this story from our colleague Greta.

Greta's Testimony

Earlier in this text, we introduced you to a Spanish teacher named Greta. Greta worked in a US high school that sat in the heart of a low socio-economic community. The student demographics included 90% minority students, most of whom were served by the free and reduced lunch program. The school faced significant challenges with student violence and apathy, to the point that it caught the federal government's attention for having disproportionate minority representation across their disciplinary data. There was deep pressure to reverse course or potentially face loss of funding.

In Greta's words, every day in her classroom was hard. The lack of food, transportation, and housing experienced by her students regularly put them on edge, and they responded to one another and to her in aggressive ways. Their lack of security in so many aspects of their lives made them edgy, tired, and skeptical of any attempt she made to build relationships with them.

To reduce annual suspensions and to better address behaviors that seemed to emerge from lives that had experienced far too much trauma, the school transitioned to a restorative justice model. But staff were not adequately prepared to introduce new classroom and school-wide strategies and activities that were in alignment with the restorative justice model (as is too often the case with new school initiatives), resulting in teacher confusion about whether the more violent, dangerous student behaviors would be exempt from the newly adopted restorative practices.

The school made an effort to apply the newly adopted alternative behavioral response approach well, but it did not work. Disciplinary numbers improved (a celebrated school victory), but violent conditions and teacher attacks escalated. Follow-through on the implementation of the new model was inconsistent, and teachers were left confused about how to introduce specific strategies and when to introduce them.

After one year of implementation with this new model, the number of violent episodes against teachers increased radically (more than eight teachers in one year were physically injured or assaulted at a faster rate than ever before, and one teacher was injured so badly by a hit to the head that she was never able to return to teaching), and teachers quit their jobs almost weekly. The school climate turned even more toxic within months.

Question for the Reader:

If your school has embraced a restorative justice model, has it had a positive impact on student behaviors and student–staff relationships?

You may be wondering at this point what happened to Greta. Well, the impact on Greta was traumatizing. Greta was left highly disillusioned, depressed, and fearful for her life. She didn't understand how her school's newly adopted framework helped traumatized students if it meant that her teaching colleagues landed in the hospital. Furthermore, she could not come to terms with the fact that students who laid hands on teachers were allowed back at school within a day or two. Where were the consequences? Asking a student to offer an apology and make amends did not seem to be effective when teaching colleagues were on IVs in hospital beds or sporting bandages or casts. We are pleased to say that Greta has remained in the classroom, albeit after leaving for a different school district in another state, but she still talks about this experience and how negatively it impacted her.

Does this mean that adopting alternative frameworks to address the impact of trauma cannot work? No, absolutely not. But what we are suggesting is that even the best-defined alternative strategies (or any strategy for that matter) for addressing trauma-induced behaviors are not easy solutions or quick fixes, and if you are going to radically change the consequences, make sure your teaching staff understands why and for what purpose so you do not lose your classroom leaders in the process of something new. Trauma is too complex of an issue to put it into a nice, neat box that only one framework can address, and we need to be open to new ideas, but only after we have prepared people to understand how to operate with the new ideas.

Greta's story reminds us that any disciplinary framework or trauma-informed strategy (whether for instruction or behaviors) requires a deep-dive, comprehensive, and adequate educator training and support framework if it is to work. It requires a significant investment from school leaders who not only support the processes but can also lead the long-term implementation of some complex models. This requires time, professional development monies, training, coaching, and retraining to ensure the processes are carried out with fidelity.

With that said, we come to an important question: What are trauma-informed strategies supposed to look like in our schools and classrooms? Consider a few markers.

Leading Our Classrooms With Trauma-Informed Care

A trauma-informed classroom is one in which "the adults in the school community are prepared to recognize and respond to those who have been impacted by traumatic stress" (Treatment and Services Adaptation Center, 2022, para. 2). If we move from this understanding to the phrase "trauma-informed instruction," then in similar fashion, we are talking about classroom practices and processes that also recognize and are prepared well to respond to students who have been impacted by traumatic stress and are thus acting in ways that can make the instructional process challenging or different. We would argue that trauma-informed classroom practice is simply practice built on the concept of care—we care about the root causes driving the behaviors we see, and we wish to create a safe environment in which students feels they can work through what is going on inside their heads and hearts without a meltdown or intense response. Trauma-aware schools and classrooms must acknowledge they cannot solve all student trauma concerns, but we agree that the trauma in a student's or staff member's life is real and worth considering.

The CDC and SAMHSA (2021) jointly developed six principles to shape a trauma-informed environment, and these six principles are highly relevant to our classrooms. They include (directly quoted from site):

♦ Safety
♦ Trustworthiness and transparency
♦ Peer support
♦ Collaboration and mutuality
♦ Empowerment and choice
♦ Cultural, historical and gender issues

If you are an advocate of the whole-child (ASCD, 2022) approach to education, these five components probably look familiar, as the whole child speaks to keeping kids safe, valued, respected, and so much more. When our youth do not feel safe and trusted or believe they cannot trust us (because the other adults in their lives have let them down or allowed them to feel unsafe), then they can unintentionally respond to school life in severe ways—largely as a way to protect themselves.

Embracing trauma-informed strategies as solutions as a regular part of daily instructional practice essentially means we are willing to initiate a more flexible approach to how we approach our learners. We allow space, time, choice, and adaptable ways to express oneself and the knowledge one has acquired or may wish to acquire. We avoid zero-tolerance approaches that impose restrictive punishments with no room for conversation. Trauma-informed teaching also recognizes that things we say or do in our classrooms can, often unexpectedly, trigger students and evoke difficult memories leading to unexplained physical behaviors. Yet we also recognize that one of our primary goals as classroom teachers is to prepare students for topics that may be hard—either academically or personally.

A common hallmark of someone who has faced trauma is a negative or potentially fixed mindset, with accompanying feelings of inadequacy. This mindset, coupled with the stress of a teacher challenging them to perform at high levels, can rapidly shut down a student's efforts. This is why building a classroom in which students have choices about how, why, and whether they answer or show knowledge is key. But saying this and doing this are two entirely different challenges.

When trauma-impacted behaviors become significantly anti-social (e.g., non-stop chatter or movement, loud outbursts, violent or aggressive behaviors that include profanity and throwing items, fights), then we are left feeling hopeless. In fact, in our conversations with teachers, the notable increase in dealing with trauma-impacted students is often reported as one reason teachers burn out quickly and leave the classroom altogether. And it is not because of the students themselves, but from the lack of resources schools provide teachers to successfully manage these relationships. What do we when all of our best strategies for behavior management feel useless?

Questions for the Reader:

Have you ever stood in front a classroom, exhausted and hopeless, thinking to yourself, "I can't do this. I don't know what to do. Nothing I try helps?" If so, how did you work through these thoughts and emotions and what were your next steps? If you could go back to that moment today, how would you confront this?

Building Your Trauma-Sensitive Knowledge: How to?

How can we educate ourselves about trauma? And what do we need to ask for in relationship to teaching trauma-impacted students in our classrooms? Trauma is a mental health concept that requires licensed mental health providers to provide deeper insight to the phenomenon and how it impacts students at school or home.

There are many ways to embrace self-study with books, streaming content, and professional development, but at the end of the day, we think it is most effective to consider engaging in a professional learning activity in which you gain the benefit of both the mental health side and the educator side (how does this impact school discipline? How does this impact school rules?). Most important, it is necessary for you to ask for and demand trauma-informed teaching and learning as part of your school's conversation.

What works for you, your students, and your community may look very different from another community, and in no way do we intend to advocate the shift to alternative approaches that fail to adequately address violent or dangerous behaviors. Nothing is a quick fix. Most important, we want you safe. We want your students safe. We want your school leaders safe. So, be patient with your own learning, consider all aspects of new information, and make sure that you and your colleagues are well informed before initiating new approaches.

Teacher Tools: Tips to Adapting New Trauma-Informed Approaches

Implementing trauma-informed practices into your classroom need not require a complete overhaul of current practices Instead, think about how routines and practices can be established that acknowledge trauma is present and the humanity of teaching and learning. Think about how these practices might fit into your classroom routines:

♦ Mindfulness
♦ Yoga, meditation, or breathing exercises
♦ Calming corners or areas for reflection
♦ Stress relievers

- ◆ Purposeful counseling availability
- ◆ Journaling or artistic expression
- ◆ Team-building exercises
- ◆ Letters to students
- ◆ Community/class meetings
- ◆ Sensory trails

Take Action! Ways Teachers Can Take Action to Build Trauma-Skilled Classrooms

1. Provide testimony to legislators proposing safe schools legislation. Support anti-bullying, smaller class sizes, and increased teacher numbers through live testimony of lived events you've witnessed.
2. Attend professional development specifically about trauma-informed practices.
3. Build a common vocabulary at your school regarding trauma and practices that build resiliency. Read more at http://dropoutprevention.org/wp-content/uploads/2018/10/Trauma-Skilled-Schools-Model-Final-I.pdf
4. Assemble resources specifically for helping teachers—that is, build coalitions specifically for teachers who might be suffering from trauma or other major life crises. Speak up about the reality that teachers suffer from trauma, too, both personally and as caretakers.
5. Offer to lead a school-based group of professionals focused on establishing stronger community partnerships with mental health organizations that work with trauma daily. Be the voice in your building that reminds everyone that it takes a village to address matters deeply entrenched in a burden of trauma.

Reflective Questions for Teachers and Leaders

1. What conversations does your school need to have to better serve traumatized students?
2. What resources are available to students and staff who have experienced trauma, and are staff ready to refer students to these resources or know how to refer them?
3. How can your school build a common language around trauma-informed practices?
4. When have you seen trauma cause behavior issues in the classroom? What ways can be built to support these types of situations?
5. What barriers are there in your school that impact students who have or are experiencing trauma?

8

Preserving and Protecting Your Reputation

Tariq was one of my 11th grade students in second block chemistry. I really liked him, and he usually did his work with no issues. But a little more than halfway through the semester, something changed. I could see that he was fidgety, quick to anger, and something was just off. Some classmates told me they thought his parents were going through a divorce and making him choose which one to live with. One day he begged me for an extra two days to finish a project, but students had already been given three weeks, and I held firm with "no." Next thing I knew, I heard that Tariq was making hurtful, false allegations about me on social media, saying I'm a mean teacher, hate Muslim students, and previously even had a DWI on my record. I never had a DWI. I didn't hate him. I don't have an issue with any religious group. It was an awful mess.

—Darnell, high school chemistry teacher

Most teachers encounter upset, angry, or grieved students in the classroom. It is just a part of being in a profession that serves people, especially when the people are not adults and have not fully formed the ability to rationalize consequences of emotional reactions. But when student anger or frustration explodes to the point that a student attempts to damage a teacher's reputation, something is seriously wrong, as a damaged reputation with potentially false allegations can all but destroy a life and career. And sadly, this is a global issue, as evidenced by the following Australian headline:

Students are using social media to ruin the reputation of schools and staff with defamatory statements. (Vonow, 2015)

DOI: 10.4324/b23214-9

Today's teachers face more than the possibility of students gossiping behind their backs at a football game. Public, easily accessible, and sometimes permanent false, untrue, misleading, or defamatory information about teachers—posted or shared by students, parents, community members, or others—seems to be one of today's most daunting professional threats.

Yet schools offer very little advice or training for teachers on how to best navigate the world of online hate. Many teachers we interviewed while writing this book reported the fear of being criticized online or falsely accused of something they did not do as a primary concern influencing their decision to be a teacher today.

Add to this repeating viral trends of students recording teachers on their mobile devices, sharing snippets of classroom outtakes (without permission), or the potential for having a conversation taken out of context, and the stakes rise. Teachers today must be constantly on guard for what they are saying, doing, and teaching—and always be under awareness that whatever they do may be recorded or shared at any given time without their knowledge or consent.

Ruining Our Reputations

In this chapter, as we explore conditions that pit teachers against teachers and students against teachers (or vice versa), we have to keep in mind that all of these unwanted outcomes hold the potential to utterly destroy a teacher's professional and personal reputation. Consequently, this is a major safe schools issue, as we want to do everything in our power to help educators avoid having their lives ruined by repeating clips on Instagram or TikTok.

With increasing reports of abuse by teachers, there is also an increase of false reports against teachers. Colorado attorney Greg Lawler told the National Education Association (NEA) (Simpson, 2006):

> Students these days know all too well the consequences of an abuse complaint, and they know how to game the system. They know how to get an unpopular teacher fired

by making false allegations, and unfortunately, some of them try to do just that.

(para.6)

As a result of the increasing growth in false claims against teachers, the NEA published a guide for new teachers that included advice like: avoid being alone with a student, keep classroom doors open, squash student crushes, be clear and concise in your rejection of student advances, and never communicate with students outside of official school email channels (Simpson, 2006).

Managing relationships is just one aspect that teachers need to do successfully. But what about when your teaching is recorded without your knowledge? Or a part of a conversation you had with a student is shared out of context (and makes you look bad)? Or what if you are purposefully set up by a student to fail? While the NEA's advice is good, it barely scratches the surface of the compounding and deeply wounding career destruction that can occur when a teacher is criticized online.

While an attack on one's professional reputation is different from an assault on one's physical body, both events are nonetheless attacks of some sort, and both hold the potential to radically alter our physical and mental well-being long term. For that reason, this chapter is dedicated to making sure your reputation, rights, and responsibilities can flourish as expected, even in the face of agitated and frustrated students, while also ensuring we maintain the same for our students.

Threats and Dangers From Students

Darnell's story shared at the start of this chapter is sadly not uncommon, as a quick Internet search of teachers who faced false or damaging allegations will result in multiple newsworthy stories. Consider this example from a British school: a student whose teacher refused to provide him a pen for an important exam (stating it was the student's responsibility to be better prepared) spent months scouring the Internet to find demeaning content to get his teacher fired. He talked to lawyers; stalked the teacher's Facebook page, looking at every picture or image he could find; researched phone numbers that had belonged to the teacher; and carefully studied online forums.

He found what he needed when he discovered the teacher had previously engaged in an online chat focused on prostitution and escorts (discovered through a search for the teacher's personal email address). After setting up a plan to draw the teacher into scheme to find escorts, the student had the scandal he needed to expose the teacher. The actions that followed the student's discovery represented nothing short of revenge. The teacher lost his job, was ruined in the press, and lost his marriage to divorce ("Teacher Refuses . . .," 2018).

Your authors do not condone this teacher's selected extracurricular activities, but the degree to which the student engaged in self-admitted, hate-driven research to purposefully do the very thing he ultimately accomplished—to destroy and ruin a teacher's life—is nevertheless shocking and sobering. Imagine if a student studied your personal life in such a passionate way. How would you feel? What would that search yield that might embarrass you or even be misconstrued as something that it is not?

This story reminds us that nothing is ever truly gone from the Internet, and things can come back to haunt us at any point. It also reminds us to make one thing very clear to you, the teacher: you will never have truly safe and secure schools if your school does not foster conditions that keep you physically, emotionally, and psychologically safe. You do not have to be struck by a bullet, slapped by a hand, or shoved accidentally during a hallway fight to experience a less than safe environment. Sometimes the very words of our students, their families, and our colleagues do more wounding damage than anything else we could imagine. This is an attack on your professionalism.

Think and Write

Consider the following scenarios and put yourself in the place of the teachers. Imagine this purposeful maligning of your good name or reputation happened to you. How would you have felt, and do you think you would have dealt with the situation well? Who would you turn to for help?

Reflect on these questions in the space below.

Think and Write Scenarios

♦ A student who received algebra tutoring assistance from his teacher spread the word that the teacher was looking "pretty hot" during tutoring and made a pass at him.

♦ A tech-savvy senior who just learned he will not graduate because he failed Ms. Horowitz's English class takes a picture of her from her Facebook page, imposes a Victoria Secret model's near-naked body on the head, and sets up a fake Internet set with a few more scantily clad models, identified as the team at "Horowitz's Hotties."

♦ A volleyball player claims that while on the school activity bus to a Tuesday night match, the coach, Mr. Relish, put his hand up the skirt of the team's water girl. By the end of the match, the news has traveled around both the home and visiting teams.

♦ While a German teacher explains the German beer brewing industry to students as part of a lesson on the German economy, a student takes a cell phone photo of an image of beer bottles, posts it to Facebook, and posts, "Look, Herr Heinz is telling us to drink beer to pass this class!"

We are not shocked when our students seek to malign our names and reputations—after all, students and schools today are more connected than ever, and they seem to be under the impression that any and all information should be shared with a global audience the second it happens. There is more access to information, more opportunity for misuse, and ample means of sharing information than we have ever experienced in our lifetimes.

We understand that students are, most likely, still evolving and maturing and may lack some restraint when things do not go their way. But we do not expect that teachers will also follow suit and engage in similar behavior, yet it does happen.

Bullying by Colleagues

While the painful or damaging words and actions of students and their parents can have long-term impacts on our emotional well-being and sense of security, damaging remarks from colleagues are perhaps even more harmful because they come from people we work alongside every day and whom we trust (ideally). When that trust is broken, our ability to engage in collaborative efforts is forever altered.

Sadly, teachers report that bullying by fellow teachers is a real phenomenon (Finley, 2013). About 24% to 46% of teachers report having been seriously bullied at work, and 89% witnessed teacher on teacher bullying at work (Mulvahill, 2019).

McEvoy (2014) explains why teacher-on-teacher abuse can infiltrate a school: power imbalances, dynamics in which teachers fear reporting others, enabling by the school system to provide sufficient reporting outlets or support, the ability of the offender to remain undetected by outsiders, or colleagues being minimized or silenced by their offender.

A growing body of educational articles that have considered teacher on teacher bullying reveal that some teachers seriously considered leaving the profession because of the way they were talked to or forced to teach like another teacher, or because of eye rolls, smirks, and snide remarks about their adopted strategies.

In fact, when *We Are Teachers* addressed this topic (Mulvahill, 2019), the authors offered teachers a Facebook support group for those who had experienced bullying from other teachers. As licensed teachers, we (Lori and Gretchen) are saddened by this trend. It is disappointing to imagine that the matter of teachers bullying teachers has grown to a point where support groups are needed. What happened to our communities of care? If we cannot trust our colleagues to treat us with care, then why should we expect anyone else to treat us in a kind manner?

Teachers face enough ridicule and heartache from the political spectrum, from the society at large, and sometimes from the students they teach, so the last thing they need is a fellow teacher holding them down and dragging their names through the mud in the teacher's lounge, grocery store, or favorite Internet site. Instead, teachers need relevant strategies on how to best prevent, confront, and defeat those that threaten their professional well-being and reputation—and they need the support of their school leadership to ensure they are not alone.

What Would You Do?

Nyah taught in a small rural elementary school for two years before making a move to a large metropolitan city with diverse cultures, languages, foods, and traditions. She wanted to work with a more diverse student population since she came from a bi-racial family and felt a calling to serve and teach students who might struggle with identity. The move to the big city seemed perfect.

Nyah had successfully used relationship-building activities with her students in the rural community and planned to continue these efforts in her new classroom. But it did not take long for other teachers on her grade-level team to criticize her efforts.

Colleagues rapidly informed her that students in this larger elementary school brought greater struggles to the table that presented in the form of aggressive or anti-social behaviors. The team suggested she "toughen up" and "get mean" with a zero-tolerance policy for all bad behaviors.

"Just send them to the principal. They need to be kicked out of our school!" was the common response when Nyah said anything about disruptive or disagreeable students.

Nyah tried to ignore the remarks and stay focused on strategies she knew would prove successful, but she nearly lost her sanity and composure when she learned that a teammate had bad mouthed her on a listserv for fifth grade teachers using her first name! Nyah was devastated and felt like a failure, deciding that she likely needed to quit the teaching profession entirely.

Question for the Reader

If you were Nyah, how would you respond to the colleague who tarnished your reputation on the listserv?

What Nyah experienced was painful and punitive, as she was being punished for employing highly recommended, research-based approaches to students in need. Had we been in her shoes, we might have felt like quitting as well. Nyah's story reminds us that even when we are doing what is right, someone may still criticize us for doing it all wrong. When this happens and we lose our peace and focus, our working environment becomes less safe and secure.

Teacher Threats to Students

So far, we have considered how our students and fellow colleagues can create hardships or impossibilities that both rob us of our job and threaten to capsize our careers, sanity, and confidence. Flip the picture for a moment and consider the reverse.

What happens when we, as teachers, become threats to those we are trusted to serve—our students? And why are we addressing this topic in this book? Because yet again, no school is safe when the chaos of negative, threatening thoughts and emotions are raging through people's minds. No amount of fire drills, active shooter drills, tornado drills, metal detectors, or school resource officers can calm, quiet, or resolve the tortured or troubled thoughts of a student who feels unsafe to learn. The same is true of adults. That is, an unwell or unstable teacher is a also threat.

Remember, we have defined school safety as the side of school that deals with the social and emotional connections we make. Do we trust those we are around? Do we believe we can talk with them openly? Do we feel physically strong to engage with those people, and do we believe they will be open to anything we might share through the course of teaching or learning?

When students lose trust in their teachers, school safety and security take a major hit. If you begin the school year with students who cannot trust their teachers, leaders, coaches, counselors, and more, it is nearly impossible to catch up. But is this really happening in schools? Sadly, yes.

Start with the most extreme example of teachers breaking trust with their students: physical or sexual assaults.

Inappropriate Student–Teacher Relationships

In 2015, slightly fewer than 500 educators in the United States were arrested for sexual misconduct. In addition, a reported 3.5 million students between grades 8 and 11 reported an experience with physical sexual conduct, most often through contact with a teacher or a coach (Sexual abuse by teachers . . ., 2017).

These are the educational data sets we don't like to admit are true, but we must consider how these experiences not only serve to traumatize students but also to destroy the classroom relationship that grounds all learning. When a student loses trust in a teacher, it can harm their educational experience for years to come while simultaneously damaging their confidence in other life relationships.

Zarra (2016) explains that multiple factors have helped foster such inappropriate relations:

> The time spent by teachers with students is increasing each year. Secondary teachers add coaching responsibilities in athletics. Added to the fixed academics, and spending time with students both at school and after school has increased. This reality places teachers with students

for additional hours throughout the day. Comparatively, this equates to more time than teachers spend with their families each night. The rise of social media and instant communications, along with a hyper-sexual American culture, tend to exacerbate the balance of moral boundaries between teachers and their charges.

(p. 16, citing Lavoie 2012, p. 2)

Zarra notes that the rise of social media has led to the possibility of greater student–teacher engagements or interactions, but social media has also led to another disturbing form of teacher–student or student–teacher attacks, namely, the threat of cyberbullying and cyberstalking.

Clearly, a relationship between a student and a teacher is unethical, immoral, and in many states, illegal, yet boundaries continue to be crossed year after year in many unsuspecting communities. Many times, we just assume that teachers will not engage in this type of behavior and often, when a teacher–student relationship is exposed, it is to the shock of disbelieving colleagues and community members.

Many school districts now include a very distinct and explicit component in their new teacher training focused on this very topic. At the end of the day, there is only one way to protect students from this type of threat: strict adherence to ethical and legal duties by all teachers in all districts, which means that districts cannot emphasize too heavily how important it is to act morally and ethically appropriate with students and stakeholders. To gain the trust of others, teachers must behave in ways that show we respect boundaries and are willing to speak up if we suspect an inappropriate relationship is taking place.

Cyber Threats: Cyberbullying and Cyberstalking

For many of us, the word "threat" invokes images of masked perpetrators, weapons, bombs, or natural disasters, but what about cyber threats—the unseen threats you never saw coming but that hold the potential to literally destroy your financial, professional, and personal life and reputation?

Web-based threats may include phishing (fake emails that when clicked give hackers access to your data or system) and system hacks that capture all sorts of data about you and your students. A tech-savvy student can take over your social media account or banking site with ease leading to financial ruin and attacks that no restraining order can stop. Consider these examples:

♦ In 2011, a North Carolina middle school teacher was charged with cyberstalking for sending repeated texts to a 13-year-old student, some of which contained sexual innuendos (Kirpalani, 2011).

♦ A Moses Lake, Washington, teacher emailed a video of an underage student engaged in a sexual act in an effort to get her removed from a school athletic team (Utter, 2020).

♦ YouTube appears to be an avenue through which students are increasingly stalking teachers by secretly recording videos during class time or creating videos that mock a teacher's mannerisms or habits (Kyriacou & Zuin, 2016).

Questions for the Reader

Have you personally or professionally ever been the victim of Internet-based fraud or scam, an act that potentially resulted in someone stealing your identity or financial information? How did that make you feel, and who did you turn to for help?

When your personal data and correspondences (emails, financial information, personal contacts) land in the wrong hands, your world can turn into chaos. Now take that sinking feeling and multiply it tenfold to understand how these cyberattacks grow more complicated when students, student data, or other stakeholders are involved. Remember that teachers and schools are expected to protect most public school student data under federal law, and any crack in the system can wreak havoc on a school. One Ohio school learned the hard way:

When Hacking and Violence Meet in the Middle: A 13-year-old Ohio teenager acquired his teacher's log-in credentials; logged into the district's student database; stole the identities of students to create a new "hit list"; and then stole 60 student names, school IDs, and birthdates from his school to establish a web-based listing of student IDs. As the student went under investigation, local law enforcement learned that the student had made prior threatening remarks, including expressing a desire to shoot up the school. School officials were left contacting the parents of the students on the hit list to notify them of the incident (Gatlan, 2013).

While the Ohio incident is an exception rather than the norm of stories about school hacks, this incident raises so many questions and concerns about student and teacher safety and security, as it highlights how one wrong act can lead to a ripple effect of larger acts that put more people and their private data in harm's way. Multiple people may lose their ability to trust the educational community when this happens.

Responding to the Rumors: Stay Quiet or Speak Up?

When attacked online or in person, through any number of imaginable avenues, a knee-jerk reaction will always be to defend yourself and immediately post a comment or speak up against your accuser. We are human, after all, and we cannot fathom false allegations ruining our names.

We might choose to yell at our colleague, an action that would put students or other staff who overhear the heated exchange on edge. We might opt to post online lies about the person who besmirched us online. Or we might choose to stay quiet and say nothing.

There are numerous ways we might respond, but if we respond in haste with aggression, anger, or revenge, then we are putting ourselves into a very volatile situation that does not keep us healthy for those we serve. That is never a good thing.

There should be a healthy inner dialogue that takes place when you consider whether to confront a rumor or to ignore it. This includes:

- ◆ The amount of damage that might be caused by the information being shared
- ◆ The potential threat to your professional reputation
- ◆ The source of the rumored information
- ◆ The likelihood that speaking up might lead to additional confrontative behaviors
- ◆ The possibility that speaking up will lead to a physical altercation
- ◆ The support you have of your colleagues and school leaders
- ◆ The timeframe and avenues needed to adequately response

When someone shares untrue or unflattering information about you either online or in person, you have to look out for yourself first. Challenge attempts by others to minimize a student spreading information as "immature" or "just what kids do." **As a professional, you should be supported to confront and correct inaccurate information and to have the peace of mind that your professional reputation is supported by your school leaders, colleagues, and students.** Accepting less or excusing this type of reputation-stealer needs to stop with you.

Your Rights in the Face of Threats

If you are starting to feel a bit anxious at this point, let us encourage you to take a deep breath and find comfort in the steps you can take to protect yourself. We do not share descriptions of potential threats to strike a chord of fear; instead, we share this information to help you effectively understand that protecting yourself and your reputation is acceptable, admirable, and recommended. Plus, the good news is that just a few simple steps can immediately strengthen your hedge of safety and security.

As teachers, we know that time is our greatest yet least available commodity, and because we get wrapped up with a million different tasks in a fast-paced and often chaotic environment, it can prove easier to say little when students or others smear our names online, attempt to hack our digital files, or spread false rumors. After all, many of us believe that if it comes down to a "he said, she said" scenario, the administrators will believe the students or parents over the teacher. Consequently, we often determine that the best and easiest approach is no approach—we stay silent.

But we are here to tell you that you cannot stay silent. Your reputation is all you really have at the end of the day, and if you lose that, you can lose your job. It is not okay to stay silent in the face of seen or unseen threats to your professional and personal life. Your mental health and physical wellness can afford your silence. Former classroom teacher Michelle knows this only too well.

Michelle's Story: Michelle taught advanced placement calculus to high school seniors on a year-long schedule. About halfway through the year, an 11th grader named Grayson grew angry, as he believed Michelle picked on him during class and assigned lower grades than he deserved on papers and projects.

One afternoon, after receiving a 70 on a paper he felt a rush of anger and decided it was time to stand up to the teacher's bullying behaviors. A few weeks prior, while driving around town, he happened to see Michelle walking out of an ABC store with two brown paper bags in hand. She had obviously purchased alcohol. Grayson took photos for future use.

The night after receiving the low grade, he returned to those photos, posting a few to Instagram with a falsified story about the wild party the teacher threw in her neighborhood, a party that some seniors supposedly attended (thus resulting in underage drinking). By 7:30 a.m. the next morning, the story landed at the feet of many students and staff members, but no one mentioned it to Michelle. She was clueless about the community-wide attacks on her name and character until she noticed people looking at her awkwardly as she walked through the hallway at the start of first period the next day. A teacher colleague quickly filled her in, and Michelle almost fainted on the spot.

Can you imagine Michelle's anger, frustration, and feeling of helplessness when she realized an angry student felt the need to release his classroom frustration through a personal attack that accused her of illegal behaviors? Michelle was purchasing wine for an upcoming holiday celebration with friends and family. No party was involved. But one picture with a false narrative ruined Michelle's name in the school community for several weeks. That was a long, hard week, a week during which Michelle could not sleep, started having physical ailments, and had to call in sick for two days in a row.

Michelle's embarrassment and anger so impacted her physical state that she grew ill and felt as if she was losing her mind. She sought medical help, and her general practitioner fortunately encouraged her to go one step further and seek counseling support to process all that had happened.

Think and Write

What can Michelle do in the face of these baseless and inaccurate rumors? Does she have the right or responsibility to engage leadership, law enforcement, or legal representation in this matter? What should she do?

Teacher Tools

Teachers do not need to remain silent in the face of their critics. Attacks, whether they come online or in person, should be acknowledged rather than ignored. However, this does not mean you should enter a debate or ongoing conversation defending your teaching or your personal life. Consider adding these questions to your teaching toolbox when thinking about dealing with your critics:

♦ Not every criticism needs a response. Listen carefully to the critic, think about the accuracy and honesty of the complaint, and assess whether it may be true. If it is, you may have room to grow and learn.

♦ If online or public allegations about you are entirely false, your first step is to contact your school administrator to discuss the situation. He/she may choose to contact the complainer (if an identity is known) to intervene and open a discussion outside of the public eye. Keep yourself willing to provide any documentation or resources the school leader could use to help address the situation.

♦ Do not meet with your accuser alone. Whether the complaint is about your teaching, your personal conduct, or your interactions with a student, always have an administrator or school leader present for the conversation. If you work within a union, you may wish to seek a union representative to join you. Document the conversation after the fact so that your recollections of the events will not fade.

♦ Responding to online criticism is generally not useful. While it may be easy to type a quick denial or to attack the attacker, remember that your online communication is forever. Even if you delete a conversation, someone somewhere can access it. Our advice is that if you do not want your words to show up on the news or be shared in an online article, never put them in writing or video.

♦ If you do choose to engage in a conversation in regard to a personal attack, keep it simple and straightforward with something like "I'd like the chance to talk to you about this. Please call our school office and set up an appointment."

♦ If you are threatened, contact law enforcement and your administrator. True threats are never protected and should not be ignored or waited out.

♦ If you are the subject of false claims that damage your reputation in measurable ways, you may need legal help.

Consider hiring an attorney or consulting your union representative to help access proper legal resources to help protect your reputation and teaching credentials.

Take Action! Standing Up Against Attacks on Your Reputation

"Dealing with" teacher critics requires more than a sassy response or simply ignoring the posts or critics. Here are five real, actionable steps you can take to use your teacher voice to amplify the presence of teachers within the conversation:

1. Inform your administrator or school leadership team in writing and in person of online conversations or avenues for public gossip. Take screenshots and share copies. Keep copies for your files. The administrator cannot legally shut down any public communication, but an awareness does trigger an administrative duty to protect teachers and their reputations. Knowledge that these things are happening is better than ignorance. Expect your school leader to establish a culture within your school where personal attacks are not part of the rituals of the school community. If your administrator can set the tone, it might silence those tempted to spout inaccurate complaints or personal attacks.

2. Maintain a professional image on social media. Yes, you have every right to chat with your friends, post on your Facebook page, or share pictures from your parties, but refrain from making all of your posts public or accessible by anyone. Do not post embarrassing, degrading photos. Do not post politically charged, racist, sexist, or derogatory posts.

3. Demonstrate that you use social media and school communications responsibly. This means not spending work time posting on social media; not complaining about your job in public chat rooms; and most definitely, not violating student privacy by

sharing information about students at all. Do not use unapproved social channels to communicate with parents or students (generally, school policies require communicating using a particular email or approved application).

4. Personally inform your administrator or school leader *in writing* when someone attacks, accuses you, or alludes to abuse by you online or in person. Share screenshots, evidence, or statements detailing the attack and indicate that you are unwilling to be bullied by parents or students. Involve a union representative when possible or consult an attorney. Demand the administrator provide you with a set of working principles on how to best navigate the situation. Ask your administrator to commit his or her support to you in writing.

5. Consult with an attorney or union representative if you sustain false attacks or charges of illegal activity or are accused of misconduct. Protect what you share with your attorney as part of your privileged conversations to protect your reputation. Your school principal does not have the right to sit in on these conversations.

Reflective Questions for Teachers and Leaders

1. Have you ever had to comfort a fellow teacher who faced a specific threat, and if so, how did it make you feel?

2. Do you know anyone who left the teaching profession because of attacks on their efforts or reputation? If so, how did it make you feel?

3. Describe how you would approach an incident in which a student has attempted to destroy your name and reputation through hateful and inaccurate social media postings.

4. What actions do you take to minimize the likelihood of accused misconduct? What personal guidelines do you adhere to that would prevent a false allegation against you?
5. How are new teachers coached and mentored on maintaining appropriate relationships with students? Who is having conversations with these teachers? Are they effective?

9

Equity as the Edge to Improved School Safety

Have you ever tried to maintain "safe and secure schools" as a special education teacher? It's not for the faint of heart. Last year I had two students who suffered meltdowns every time the monthly fire alarm went off. It was all but impossible to get them to evacuate the classroom. And a physics teacher down the hall from me had a female student (Natalia) who had suffered traumatic physical abuse as a child by being locked in a closet, so every two months when we had an active shooter drill and had to force kids to hide under desks, in closets, and in bathrooms, this student would melt down and start screaming. Please tell me how we're supposed to complete drills when this is the reality of student needs!

—Kara, sixth grade teacher

Equitable mindsets and practices foster and maintain safe and secure schools, and for this reason, we end this text with a final important emphasis on grounding all our safe and secure school efforts on a foundation of equitable approaches, responses, and understandings.

Establishing caring, trusting, open, and flexible environments in which we believe our students will listen to us, trust us, and remain flexible to move with us to more secure locations in the face of real threats is only possible if we acknowledge that each student potentially needs something different to reach that place.

"Equity" is an oft used term in educational circles, but it is sadly misunderstood. Equity is not equality. Equity does not imply that we give every student the same environment, the

DOI: 10.4324/b23214-10

same drills, the same precautions about how to stay safe and secure, and the same rules or disciplinary responses. In fact, equity has nothing to do with giving every person the same of anything. Instead, equity is about giving each individual student or stakeholder what he/she needs to thrive and remain safe and secure, and this may look very different from person to person.

The Glossary of Education Reform (Great Schools Partnership, 2016) defines equity as follows:

> In education, the term equity refers to the principle of fairness. While it is often used interchangeably with the related principle of equality, equity encompasses a wide variety of educational models, programs, and strategies that may be considered fair, but not necessarily equal. It has been said that "equity is the process; equality is the outcome," given that equity—what is fair and just—may not, in the process of educating students, reflect strict equality—what is applied, allocated, or distributed equally.
>
> (para. 1)

This definition explains that while the end result may be the same (equal outcomes = all students are safe), the way we reach this outcome may be different and unique based on each person's unique needs. As teachers, we understand that some students need constant verbal feedback, while others prefer quiet, only to be rewarded with a positive end grade showing success. How we convey to students that they did the right or wrong thing differs from student to student because we are unique beings. Safe and secure processes force us to think about individual needs with equitable avenues of success.

Consider Kara's story from our chapter introduction. Whereas many students might evacuate quickly in the face of a loud, blaring fire alarm, one student could not make this move because the chaos of the loud noise and bright flashing light from the hallway alarm was too much to take in. So, what was Kara's school doing for that student? While fire drills need to be unannounced events, was it worth shocking this student into a monthly meltdown that left him immobile while building was properly evacuated?

Could that teacher and student be given a friendly warning so they could evacuate early and move farther away from a trigger?

Now, think about our student, Natalia, and the way that active shooter drills, which demanded teachers hide their students from potential intruders, triggered horrendous memories of a painful and traumatic childhood experience of abuse and being locked inside a dark closet for long periods of time while her parents focused on their own needs. How is Natalia's school addressing this frequent trigger and making the act of a safe school drill more manageable and less triggering?

Last, revisit the needs of Kara and her physics teacher colleague down the hall. How will they feel when confronted with triggers that they knew would result in their students facing past or current traumas all over again? After all, if their own students would not evacuate or hide, then what will they do when a real threat appears? Inevitably, the teacher and students would have become easy targets or been trapped by spreading flames.

There is just something about being a teacher that makes us try everything in our power to make sure we never leave even one student behind or in harm's way, but when making sure we leave no one behind means we are putting ourselves in the way of a distinct, real threat, we cannot help but wonder if there's not a better solution. Or, to put it another way, we ask: Does the need to keep the entire school safe and secure trump the need of these individual students who are endangered or triggered negatively by safe and secure practices?

In this chapter, we dive into this challenging topic to determine how equitable approaches really can give us an edge in the face of needing to keep our learning communities completely safe and secure. To do this, we need to first start with our own perceptions and challenges as teachers.

Understanding Our Own Perceptions as Teachers

Teaching is fundamentally a human service: we work directly with and for other people, we care for and about them, and we live and work within a school community of others who may have vastly different lived experiences than we do. However, as professionals, we are expected to set aside differences and bring our students together as a whole group—one that can accomplish academic tasks and content within a similar setting. This does not mean that their (or our) individual differences disappear; rather, it requires us to learn to work together and acknowledge that our differences can coexist while we learn.

But embedded in this human-focused endeavor, we bring our own ideas, challenges, and perceptions with us as we attempt to keep our students safe. This means that we may hold or exhibit biases, perceptions, stereotypes, and even unintended discriminatory practices that influence how we work with our students. This, in turn, may influence how we feel about safety in our classrooms. Consider these different aspects that can interfere with how we perceive our students:

- ◆ **Biases:** Bias exists when we pay attention to or emphasize one aspect of a student's life or background more than another's. For instance, a teacher may hold a bias against a student who wears gang-affiliated clothing to school.
- ◆ **Prejudices:** Prejudice is "pre-judging" someone, whether we have actual experience to support our opinion. A teacher may be prejudiced against student athletes because of the perception that they do not achieve as high as other students.
- ◆ **Discrimination:** Discrimination is when we act on our prejudices and treat someone differently because of how we perceive them to be. Historically, public schools in the United States discriminated against Black students by mandated segregated schooling.
- ◆ **Oppression:** Oppression is unjust treatment of someone. A group of immigrant students may find themselves oppressed or silenced because they fear their parents' illegal immigrant status may be discovered by their peers or teachers.
- ◆ **Power:** Power is the position of authority or influence nearly every teacher holds. Regardless of how democratic

you hope to build your classroom, there will always be a power dynamic at play between adults and minors and teachers and students.

◆ **Privilege:** Privilege is an advantage someone has that others may not. For instance, students who attend a school with a massive budget may have the privilege of access to newer technology and more experienced teachers than students in school with a minimal budget.

This is more than a list of definitions. In each of these arenas, teachers face the potential of misreading, misunderstanding, or mistakenly assuming things about their students that may or may not be true. In this, the teacher may abuse their power differential (using power as a way to hide a fear of an unstable student) or may make assumptions about students from different cultures, communities, or backgrounds.

Safety does not mean treating every student the same regardless of who they are or how they behave. Instead, it requires us, as teachers, to acknowledge that we walk into our classrooms as humans with presuppositions about others. We may be afraid of students who are from neighborhoods where violence is taking place. We may misunderstand the intentions of students from different cultures. And we may simply not be aware that some students have faced lifetimes of oppression, silencing, and bias from their teachers.

Instead of defending ourselves, we are better to admit that we hold biases, stereotypes, and privileges that our students may not ever experience. We can actively reflect on how our own educational experiences may be vastly different and how our cultural background may conflict with that of our students. This does not mean we expect less or diminish rigor; rather, we approach safety as a shared concern with our students—that regardless of who we are, where we call home, or what we look like, we all deserve to be safe in our classroom together. This means, as teachers, we must recognize that part of safety is acknowledging that in our roles we may hold inherent predispositions to our students that we need to overcome.

Equity Excuses

It is common for parents to ask why one school has access to select programs, initiatives, safeguards, practices, or opportunities and another school less than 10 miles down the road has no access to the same. This is particularly true in safe and secure school practices and opportunities. Why does one school have a metal detector and another does not? Why does one school have a full time school resource officer and another does not? The answers we offer to these questions can unfortunately push us into excuses that fail to address the differences. Consider the following excuses:

- ◆ "That school sits in a really violent community, so they need more equipment and technology to stay safe. . ."
- ◆ "The parents in this community don't care if we don't do the drills, so we've just got other things to attend to than these useless drills. . ."
- ◆ "That won't happen here, so we don't need to take precautions. . ."
- ◆ "It's just the local culture. We can't fix it or prevent its negative impact on our safety. . ."

Among these excuses that could be used to explain why a school fails to provide highly personalized safe and secure supports for students and staff, perhaps none is more shocking than the one that starts with the premise of "that will never happen here." If you ask most victims of mass school shootings whether they ever imagined someone might bring a gun to campus, many will likely explain they initially thought their school or community was safe at one time early in their career. But many will also tell you that they had a gut feeling something might happen because they knew when students just were not themselves. They watched things go from bad to worse.

Furthermore, violence and threats know no boundaries. No school is immune to the potential for someone considering a targeted act of violence to act on that desire and engage in deadly or dangerous behaviors. We must believe that anything can happen anywhere, so the need to regularly maintain proactive principles and practices for safe and secure school is never optional.

While we understand that funding and community demands play a part in the extent to which schools embrace and practice safe school activities and develop safe and secure school conditions, we do not believe that any school can hide behind money or community expectations or assumptions. These influences cannot and should not be the sole reason why something isn't done or promoted.

Increased funding alone does not make any school safer or more secure because safe schools are largely about the social emotional connections we make with learners. Do students trust us to keep them safe and to confide in us about potential threats? Are we able to spend enough quality time with them in the classroom to notice a change in behavior or personality? Are we communicating with their parents or support system? No amount of money can create that reality. But educational funding and the physical resources or trainings or services purchased with said funding must be embraced with a purposeful intention to establish the optimal environment for each learner. Consider this:

If one group of students (e.g., a migrant population that escaped physical and emotional trauma) needs a smaller classroom environments to feel safer but another group of students needs to see adult monitors on school buses to feel protected from student bullying, then as teachers we have a responsibility to advocate for funds to be used in purposeful ways to make these conditions a reality. We are the ones most likely to witness these issues and the first to be able to clearly represent the issue to school leaders.

We acknowledge that there is never enough funding for all that we desire in schools, particularly when it involves funding people and additional positions. Funding school bus monitors to prevent bullying behaviors is a wise idea that likely will not gain much traction in many districts because the funds cannot sustain these positions for the long term.

But to assume that we cannot implement a solution because of limited funds or because the population needing this solution is too small to worry about (meaning we assume their safety needs are not as important as those of the larger student body) is wrong and undermines the very idea that we want equitable safe and secure practices. The needs of the 150 or 200 students who feel unsafe on the school bus are as critical as the needs of your 1,500 9th to 12th grade students who engage in a monthly fire drill. Equity means we find a solution for the bus riders and the fire drill students. Small numbers should never mean inequitable choices.

Equity Enablers

If equitable safe and secure school practices means we provide each student and teacher the right supports and opportunities to feel and trust they are safe and secure in our buildings, then how do we enable that reality when so many voices are clamoring for attention and funding? How do we commit to finding and employing the right solutions, without excuse, when funds are limited, needs are large, and our energy is waning? We must enable our people to become equity advocates in the larger picture of safety and security. Consider these examples:

- Empower student leaders to become conversation starters— to engage other students in talking about what they need to feel safer and more secure.
- Invite staff members to bring student or community identified concerns about unsafe practices to monthly meetings so a key leadership team can address before concerns result in crises.
- Establish a school-wide mindset that says every teacher or every classroom may not receive the same funding or supports. (We know this is tough, but equity demands we acknowledge some classrooms and populations present greater needs than others.)
- Permit grade or subject area teacher teams to identify the students or populations whose safe and secure school needs appear to be unnoticed, including reasons why some students do not feel safe at the bus stop, in the

restroom or cafeteria, or in other areas of the school or times of day.

- Enable teachers to become "climate and culture" practitioners who take the findings of school climate audits and work to identify best practice solutions.
- Expand opportunities for community-based mental health supports to better address the needs of students whose silent worries and fears prevent improved safety.

This list can continue to grow with your inputs and ideas. In fact, take a moment and add your ideas in the box. Describe one or two ways your school can empower and enable you and your fellow teachers and students to improve unequitable conditions:

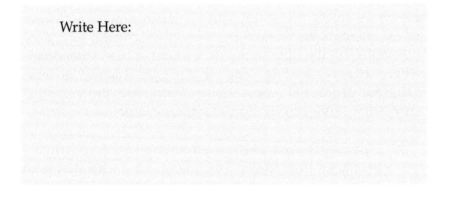

Write Here:

Inviting students and teachers to identify inequitable conditions that threaten optimal safety and security is in and of itself one of the best safe school measures you can take. Too often we believe that safer and more secure schools are about more gadgets, more drills, more places to hide, and better locking windows and doors. But in reality, the best preventive measure for a truly safe school is a school that has developed a culture and classroom climate that screams: "You matter. Your needs matter. You are a priority. We need and want to hear your voice." **Empowered voices are active ones that see the bigger picture and provide district and school leaders with the types of input needed to identify effective practices.**

Educating Others on Equity

One of the most significant challenges you will face as you help your school and district embrace a fully equitable approach to safe and school schools is the anger that emerges when people begin to understand that responses or opportunities are not "equal," and that is perfectly okay.

Equitable safety and security practices could result in the following outcomes:

- ◆ A teacher who lived through the experience of a community-based drive-by gang shooting is too nervous to return to school where other gang members attend school and is allowed to take a leave of absence. Another teacher who has requested a leave of absence to address minor family concerns is not granted leave.
- ◆ Students who are triggered by loud alarms or drills are allowed to exit or evacuate prior to a drill to prevent dangerous meltdowns. All other students follow a prescribed path.
- ◆ Alternate evacuation pathways are designed for students in wheelchairs, while mobile students follow a predetermined path.
- ◆ A social-emotional or character-building coach is hired to work with select students or small groups of students, meaning everyone in the school does not gain access to this coach. Some students with mental health issues do not receive access to a coach.
- ◆ Some older classrooms with outdated windows receive highly specialized locking and unlocking devices on doors or windows to make the evacuation process faster, while others are placed on a staggered plan for replacement over the next five years.
- ◆ Instead of funds being used to provide all teachers with a safety workshop for continuing education unit credits, a select small group is sent to a national safe schools conference. Some teachers do not receive this training initially because the core group takes the time to establish itself as the "experts" who teach their fellow teachers.

- ◆ A classroom in a mobile trailer that is disconnected from the main school building receives a fully installed radio and walkie talkie system in order to improve contact with the main school office and administrators, while classrooms within the building utilize a built-in intercom system.
- ◆ The school counseling team pulls together a small support group of English Language Learners students who feel less safe than their peers because they do not yet have full English language proficiency and are sometimes mocked or do not understand directions during drills. This places them at a disadvantage in efforts to keep themselves safe.

As you note with these examples, equitable approaches to safer and more secure schools mean that we prioritize needs, funding, and resources in a way that provides each person what she/he needs to feel safer and more secure. And let's be honest—what your students need to feel safe in a building may be very different from what you need, as our histories, philosophies, experiences, and beliefs shape the extent to which we all feel safe.

I (Lori) will never forget a time when I felt threatened by a student. What I needed in that season of my career to feel safe and free from attack was for the student to receive mental health supports to address deep anger and rage that I sensed any time I had dialogue with the student. I wondered whether a school expulsion would be allowed to permit the student to obtain more residential or hospital-based supports. After months of worry, the student's family was able to obtain a higher level of care for the student in a hospital setting, but before that happened, I walked around in fear, looking over my shoulder, wondering if the student was going to say or do something else out of anger or rage. I was very vulnerable, and it was not a pretty feeling.

Now, is this example provided to advocate for just suspending or expelling any student who makes us feel unsafe? No. But this example explains something that nobody understood. My engagement with this student left me deeply troubled, and while I expressed concerns about the student's behavior, I never truly said, "Hey! I'm scared he/she is going to hurt me!" because in my mind, that was admitting too much vulnerability and could make it appear that I had no idea what I was doing in my school. I let my ego blind me to the need for my school to provide me with equitable supports so that I did not feel threatened. I hope you will not be so quiet when or if you face this situation.

Unfortunately, we remain so hyperfocused on what our students need to feel safe that we often forget to ask what each teacher, leader, coach, counselor, and teacher assistant needs to feel safe and secure. This means we have a clear need to educate ourselves and colleagues about equitable endeavors for safer schools.

Questions for the Reader

Think about the steps your school has taken to keep you and students safe and secure. Can you identify anyone or any group of persons who you believe are not being heard well and may be more vulnerable to threats? Write about your observations below and identify one step you can take to make this known to school leadership.

Write Here:

The Dangers of Equal Safe School Supports

As noted, equality is different from equity. In the world of safe and secure schools, it is not uncommon for schools to assume that every student or teacher needs the same thing to be safer and more secure. Every student needs drills. Every student needs a safe school assembly at the start of the year. Every teacher needs a door without a window. Every teacher needs a weapon. But we recommend the opposite. Yes, sometimes keeping our schools safe and secure means everybody gets the same preparations, but this is never a catch all for school safety.

Perhaps nowhere do we see this more than in schools that choose to adopt a one-size-fits-all zero-tolerance policy towards student discipline. These policies tend to do more harm than good, as they can result in a young student with a butter knife being suspended for having a weapon on campus or can mean that a student who accidentally knocked another student down the stairs is suspended for causing a physical assault.

The circumstances and conditions around unsafe behaviors vary from school to school and from classroom to classroom. What one school perceives as a weapon another may see as a regular part of a kid's lunch box. When we argue for and promote a one-size-fits-all approach to our responses to the unexpected, we are indirectly stating that we do not support equitable practices for those we serve. If we know that suspending a student means his/her parent will beat them to the point of harm or that forcing a student to complete a safety drill will add to his/her personal trauma, then why would we force these outcomes?

The same is true of our teachers. If we know that a teacher needs a strong mentor teacher to be safer and more secure in their daily practice and outcomes, then why would we ever deny that request just because we do not have enough mentor teachers to provide every teacher with one?

Too often in education we let funding and fears of what others may think stop us from thinking outside of the box or from taking highly unpopular steps (e.g., mandating every door to the building remain locked all day), but the result of these fears is inequity. How do we reverse these trends and find the courage to do what is different, even if it means people make false assumptions about our practices? We expand our networks. We talk to teachers and leaders who have embraced the non-traditional equitable approaches, even if it means they risked their reputations and their role in the profession to make something happen.

In more recent years, we have heard about schools placing washing machines and clothes dryers in their builders so that students without access to these machines can get their clothes washed and avoid missing school. In fact, one school that utilized this approach saw increased attendance when students had access to available laundry equipment. No textbook list of effective school conditions includes a washer and dryer, but the schools that have embraced this choice have done so with the intent to meet all student needs. That is how we must think about equitable safe school practices. If some of our students or teachers need highly targeted mental health supports to reduce volatility and to improve their ability to show resilience and trust the staff, then we should do everything we can to find a way to make this possible, even if it means we explore non-traditional funding sources.

To help prioritize an equitable (instead of an equal) approach to comprehensive safe and secure practices, we recommend embracing a schoolwide equity edict. This edict can serve as a daily reminder that everything you face today or tomorrow needs to be considered and explored through one central question: "What does each student and teacher in this building need to teach and learn?

Tool: Sample Equity Edict

Equity Edict

At _____ School, we pledge to:

- Honor the unique needs and desires of all school community members.
- Address problems or conditions through multiple perspectives.
- Engage students and teachers in the identification of solutions.
- Regularly engage all voices, with a focus on those traditionally underserved.
- Promote practices that ensure no voice or need is left unheard.
- Refrain from one-size-fits-all solutions.

◆ Exercise courage and bravery in the face of difficult or unpopular decisions.

◆ Establish safe and secure school practices that promote equitable opportunities for and conditions around every person's need to feel safe and secure.

Take Action: Ways Teachers Can Speak Up for Equity

1. Seek out opportunities to understand the nuances and challenges of equity-based practices. Ask for these as professional development options and attend these regularly.

2. Work to understand your school and district's budget processes. Learn why money is spent and where it is allocated. As you see inequities or opportunities to strengthen teacher resources, identify these to your leadership team and district leaders. Use specific evidence from budgeting processes to illustrate your points.

3. Identify opportunities to be an "equity advocate" in your building and district. When speaking up about issues of discipline, numbers, resources, or teacher support, frame these issues as equity issues, not just personal complaints or wish list items. Consider making this a formal teacher leadership role.

4. Make lists of observations and concerns you hear from students, community members, and fellow teachers. Use this list to provide specific evidence (without naming names) of the real-life concerns shared with you as someone promoting an equitable learning environment.

5. Practice speaking up about equity. Capture one or two personal experiences that clearly illustrate there are climate or culture issues in your building and offer at least one specific solution to each of these issues. Use this as an elevator speech to school

leaders, at board meetings, or in community groups to demonstrate the reality of working in your school and the opportunity for change to improve conditions.

Reflection Questions for Teachers and Leaders

1. Do you believe that your colleagues understand the difference between equity and equality? Where do you hear these words mentioned in your daily conversations?

2. To help you feel safer and more secure in your building, what might your school leadership need to do that is different from how they respond to other teacher needs?

3. Have you heard others make excuses for a lack of safe and secure practices or responses? If so, what were those responses and how did you respond?

4. Place yourself into the school leader's shoes: Assume you have a group of 75 middle school students who are protesting the bi-monthly active shooter drills because these drills scare them. How do you equitably respond to the safe and secure school needs of these 75 students, knowing that your district has mandated completion of the drills?

5. Generate ideas to empower and enable you, your colleagues, and students to advocate for stronger, more equitable safe school practices.

10

Epilogue

As we prepare the final touches for this book, reflecting on the safe and secure school strategies, tips, and tools embedded across the chapters, we realize just how much schools and the crises they face have changed dramatically just in the past few years. The new normal of the post-COVID world was anything but normal, and we are left acknowledging that matters of school safety and security are evolving by the day, if not by the minute. This reality has left teachers scrambling to adapt and evolve to new responsibilities, expectations, and norms. Yet teacher voices remain silenced or rarely used to forge ahead in this new frontier.

We began this book knowing that too many teacher voices were silenced or never acknowledged and that it was not just students or their parents who potentially felt unsafe or unsecure at school. We knew, because we saw firsthand, that many teachers and other school staff were regularly in the face of unsafe environments or conditions. Because of this, it is important that your voice is **heard** and that your voice and mind are invited to think, formulate, and articulate the challenges and opportunities that live in your classroom, while also finding ways to advocate for and speak up for your needs.

Think about the danger of ignoring the voices, experiences, and thoughts of teachers. What does this mean? First, ignoring your voice means our professional standing is diminished. If we allow others to tell us what we should think or believe about education

DOI: 10.4324/b23214-11

and matters of safety or security, we lose our autonomy and the ability to know what is true from our daily work with our students. We become pawns in political battles for funding and resources.

Second, silent or ignored teacher voices means people (e.g., politicians) who potentially do not understand student development, the nature of learning, or the dynamics of everyday life in a school are making decisions without personal knowledge of the impact of those decisions. Think about the politician at your state level or in Washington, DC, deciding when and how you teach a particular subject or determining what resources your students are entitled to have with funds allocated to schools. The best way to avoid becoming a pawn in someone else's decision-making process is to have a seat at the decision-making table, so our voice needs to be there.

Last, we diminish our professional integrity when we remain silent. Following the tragic mass shooting at Virginia Tech in 2007, Professor and English Department Chair Lucinda Roy wrote a book titled *No Right to Remain Silent: The Tragedy at Virginia Tech*, about her challenging teaching experience with the shooter, as well as the surreal experience of living through a mass shooting. In the forward to her text, Roy argues that in many cases, when we see the red flags around our students and we just know something is off or we sense we could be facing danger, it is easier to remain silent. Although speaking specifically of the higher education world, her words ring true for K-12, as she writes:

> The focus on an individual's privacy and confidentiality in higher education is sometimes so exclusive that it can exclude the welfare of everyone else. Often, people who report their concerns are ultimately left to deal with the issue themselves because, even when there are good people around trying their best to offer assistance, the legal, institutional, and personal ramifications associated with intervention are daunting.
>
> (Roy, 2009, p. 8)

Much like Roy, we are often left to deal with the challenging red flags in our schools, not sure that anybody can really help us and worried about the ripple effects of pushing things too far. And so, we stay silent, although, in Roy's words, we have no right to remain silent because our safety and professional integrity matter, too.

At the end of the day, as educators, we are also everyday humans who feel things deeply. The care and compassion we practice daily is not always easy, especially when red flags are going off around a student, family, or other staff members with whom we engage through the course of our work. There are days when we want to walk away entirely and other days when we know that we are part of a transformative profession. Sometimes this comes with a great deal of sacrifice on our parts—our own mental health and well-being, time with our families, and the longevity of our career paths. By not insisting on participating in decision-making processes on school safety and security, we let others assume we have no opinion on these matters. We continue to be ignored, taken advantage of, and even slighted.

Your safety and security in your job matters because YOU matter. As more safety gadgets, processes, drills, and rules are periodically implemented and eventually discarded, you remain present with your students doing what you do best. You hear the banter in the news of politicians wanting more gun laws, stricter school rules, and more enhanced school security, yet you go on teaching, planning, and guiding your students. And you rapidly notice when the conversations about safe schools and classrooms lead to final decisions in which your classroom reality was never considered.

Speaking up is frightening. Speaking up about safety is even scarier because much about school safety leads to political debates we would prefer to avoid. When it comes to matters of school security and personal and emotional safety, there is, unfortunately, not always a clear right and wrong or safe and unsafe choice because of the very concerns Roy (2009) highlights—legal rights, individual privacy, Health Insurance Portability and Accountability Act and Family Educational Rights and Privacy Act legislation, and so much more.

Additionally, speaking up sometimes means speaking out against our employer or community, and that is something that we always want to handle with grace and dignity, as we understand that many of our leaders **do** have our best interests at heart. We applaud the thousands of leaders and directors working alongside teachers every day to keep conditions optimal and to hear teacher complaints, concerns, and crises.

But there are many people, both inside and outside of the field of education, who do not understand our current reality. Thus, we really need your voice of experience to tell the story of what it is like to enter a classroom of unknowns, to build relationships with students who have lived years of trauma, or to be so drained at the end of a day of dealing with classroom management that your own well-being is ignored. Because your safety and security matter as much as anybody else's, we cannot allow leaders, legislators, or lawsuits to ignore your needs or to dictate how you work best in your own classroom, just as much as we never want to ignore the voices of leaders and legislators who fight hard for our needs. Now, more than ever, we need your voice to be present.

What does "speaking up" mean in today's world? It means

- Asking questions of your elected officials
- Writing letters to Congressional members detailing how school safety legislation impacts student learning
- Sharing the lessons you've learned as you've dealt with problematic students with your school leaders
- Not hiding your opinion when school discussions focus on matters of safety and security
- Being present at board meetings or in committee sessions when discussions about school district policies are changing
- Letting school leaders know when school policies are interrupting or disrupting their learning
- Respectfully standing up to your administrators when they are promoting practices that make your classroom less safe

We challenge you to trust your instinct and professional judgment and use your expertise to advocate for not only you, but every other teacher doing what you do every day.

As experienced teachers, we know better than anyone that we are sometimes far too nice. It is inherent in our nature somehow to be nice, agreeable people. But it is time, amid all of the issues, challenges, and pitfalls we discuss in this book, to ensure that teacher voice carries as much weight as student and other stakeholder voices as we begin to re-create what a safe and secure school looks like. To do this, we must be willing to speak up, insist on being treated as the professionals that we are, and expect to be respected for our judgment.

We are grateful you've invested your time in this book. As educators and authors, we are passionate about listening to and advocating for teachers and their safety, and we hope you'll continue this conversation with us long after this book reaches your doorstep. Because we are teachers supporting teachers, we often lead professional development sessions that include engaging discussions on topics surrounding school safety and the teacher's voice. Please feel free to reach out to us anytime to discuss opportunities for further learning or just to share your experiences with the content of this book. We are serious when we say we want to hear from you! We believe in you and hope you find strength from our work. And remember . . . be safe, make sure you're secure, and take care of you because you are an amazing professional.

References

American Psychological Association. (2020). *Trauma*. American Psychological Association. Retrieved from www.apa.org/topics/trauma/

Andrews, N. (2019, November 4). *Mold, rodent droppings, extreme temperatures: Connecticut's schools are falling apart and making students and teachers sick*. Connecticut Education Association. Retrieved from https://blogcea.org/2019/11/04/mold-rodent-droppings-extreme-temperatures-connecticuts-schools-are-falling-apart-and-making-students-and-teachers-sick/

ASCD. (2022). *The ASCD whole child approach to education: Connect the dots to your students' success*. Association for Supervision and Curriculum Development. Retrieved from www.ascd.org/whole-child

Barnes, S. (2019, November 24). Teacher confessions: A student threatened to kill me and was in my class the next day. *Indy K-12*. Retrieved from https://indy.education/2019/11/24/teacher-confessions-a-student-threatened-to-kill-me-and-was-in-my-class-the-next-day/

Barshay, J. (2019, May 6). The promise of "restorative justice" starts to falter under rigorous research. *The Hechinger Report*. Retrieved from https://hechingerreport.org/the-promise-of-restorative-justice-starts-to-falter-under-rigorous-research/?utm_source=feedburner&utm_medium=feed&utm_campaign=Feed%3A+HechingerRepor t+%28Hechinger+Report%29

Blad, E., & Will, M. (2019, March 24). "I felt more traumatized than trained": Active-shooter drills take toll on teachers. *Education Week*. Retrieved from www.edweek.org/ew/articles/2019/03/24/i-felt-more-traumatized-than-trained-active-shooter.html

Brown, L., & Buskey, F. (2014). Creative crisis: The testimony of English teachers confronted with violent writing. *Journal of Adolescent and Adult Literacy*, 58(1), 37–47. http://doi.org/10.1002/jaal.321

Cascade Behavioral Health. (2022). *Mental and behavioral health: Symptoms, signs, & effects of psychological trauma*. Retrieved from www.cascadebh.com/behavioral/trauma/signs-symptoms-effects/

Catone, K., & Saunders, M. (2018, May 31). Teacher leadership and advocacy for policy, equity, & justice. *Center for policy, research, and evaluation*. Retrieved from https://research.steinhardt.nyu.edu/site/metroblog/2018/05/31/teacher-leadership-and-advocacy-for-policy-equity-justice/

CDC and SAMHSA. (2021). *6 guiding principles to a trauma-informed approach*. Retrieved from www.cdc.gov/cpr/infographics/6_principles_trauma_info.htm

Center on Positive Behavior Intervention. (2022). *What is PBIS?* Center on Positive Behavior Intervention (PBIS). Retrieved from www.pbis.org/pbis/getting-started

Centers for Disease Control and Prevention. (n.d.). *Fact sheet: Coping with a traumatic event*. Centers for Disease Control. Retrieved from www.cdc.gov/masstrauma/factsheets/public/coping.pdf

Centers for Disease Control and Prevention: Center for Preparedness and Response. (2022). *Infographic: 6 guiding principles to a trauma-informed approach*. Centers for Disease Control and Prevention. Retrieved from www.cdc.gov/cpr/infographics/6_principles_trauma_info.htm

Centers for Disease Control and Prevention: National Center for Injury Prevention and Control, Division of Violence Prevention. (2021). *Fast fact: Preventing youth violence*. Retrieved from www.cdc.gov/violenceprevention/youthviolence/fastfact.html

Centers for Disease Control and Prevention: National Center for Injury Prevention and Control, Division of Violence Prevention. (2021). *Preventing bullying fact sheet*. Retrieved from www.cdc.gov/violenceprevention/pdf/yv/Bullying-factsheet_508_1.pdf

Chandler, M. A. (2017). Sesame Street launches tools to help children who experience trauma, from hurricanes to violence at home. *The Washington Post*. Retrieved from www.washingtonpost.com/news/inspired-life/wp/2017/10/07/sesame-street-launches-tools-to-teach-coping-skills-to-children-who-experience-trauma-of-all-kinds-from-natural-disasters-to-violence-at-home/

Chuck, E., Johnson, A., & Siemaszko, C. (2018, February 14). *17 killed in mass shooting at high school in Parkland, Florida*. Retrieved from www.nbcnews.com

Clinton, W. J. (1999). *President Clinton's remarks regarding Columbine school shooting* [video file]. Retrieved from www.youtube.com/watch?v=sQX8KNXP14w

Colorado Department of Education. (n.d.). *School safety audit checklist.* Retrieved from www.cde.state.co.us/

Comer, J. P. (1988). Is 'parenting' essential to good teaching? *NEA Today,* 6, 34–40.

Connecticut Education Association. (2018, March 14). *Connecticut education association statement: Rise in aggressive student behavior in the classroom impacting students, teachers.* Retrieved from www.cea.org/issues/press/2018/mar/14/rise-in-aggressive-student-behavior-in-the-classroom-impacting-students-teachers.cfm

Davis, M. (2015, October 29). Restorative justice: Resources for schools. *Edutopia.* Retrieved from www.edutopia.org/blog/restorative-justice-resources-matt-davis

Dickinson, T. (2019, March 21). Mock executions? Real screams and blood? Just another school shooter drill. *Rolling Stone.* Retrieved from www.rollingstone.com/politics/politics-news/teachers-injured-active-shooter-drill-811383/

Dwyer, K. (2019, February 14). Guns in school? Here's a list of states that allow armed teachers. *McCall.* Retrieved from www.mcall.com/news/education/mc-nws-guns-in-schools-list-20181108-story.html

Educators for Excellence. (2018). *Voices from the classroom: A survey of America's educators.* Retrieved from https://e4e.org/sites/default/files/2018_voices_from_the_classroom_teacher_survey.pdf#page29

Fast, J. (2009). *Ceremonial violence: Understanding Columbine and other school rampage shootings.* New York, NY: Abrams Press.

Finley, T. (2013). In their own words: Teachers bullied by colleagues. *Edutopia.* Retrieved from www.edutopia.org/blog/teachers-bullied-by-colleagues-1-todd-finley

Gatlan, S. (2013, March 21). 13-year-old allegedly hacked teacher account to create student "Hit List." *Bleeping Computer.* Retrieved from www.bleepingcomputer.com/news/security/13-year-old-allegedly-hacked-teacher-account-to-create-student-hit-list/

Great Schools Partnership. (2016). Equity. In *The glossary of education reform.* Great Schools Partnership. Retrieved from www.edglossary.org/equity/#:~:text=In%20education%2C%20the%20term%20

equity%20refers%20to%20the,may%20be%20considered%20
fair%2C%20but%20not%20necessarily%20equal

Grinberg, E., & Muaddi, N. (2018, March 26). How the Parkland students pulled off a massive national protest in only 5 weeks. *CNN*. Retrieved from www.cnn.com/2018/03/26/us/march-for-our-lives/index.html

Grossman, K. (2015, July 6). What schools will do to keep students on track. *The Atlantic*. Retrieved from www.theatlantic.com/education/archive/2015/07/chicago-graduation-rates/397736/

Gutierrez, I. (2019, November 18). Almost a dozen Hartford schools could contain dangerous PCBS. *NBC Connecticut*. Retrieved from www.nbcconnecticut.com/investigations/over-a-dozen-hartford-schools-could-contain-dangerous-pcbs/2152060/

Hall, P., & Souers, K. (2016). *Fostering resilient learners: Strategies for creating a trauma-sensitive classroom*. ASCD. Retrieved from www.thewash-ingtonexaminer.com

Hannigan, J., & Hannigan, J. E. (2016). *Don't suspend me: An alternative discipline toolkit*. Thousand Oaks: Corwin.

Jones, S. (2018, February 21). Why school leaders fake academic success. *The Conversation*. Retrieved from https://theconversation.com/why-school-leaders-fake-academic-success-91034

Jordan, H. (2020). *What makes a school safe? End zero tolerance*. Retrieved from www.endzerotolerance.org/single-post/2018/12/05/Rethinking-School-Safety

Kelmon, J. (2014, October 30). When the teacher is the bully. *Great-Schools.org*. Retrieved from www.greatschools.org/gk/articles/when-the-teacher-is-the-bully/

Kirpalani, R. (2011, June 24). Teacher charged with cyberstalking roils North Carolina Town. *ABC News*. Retrieved from https://abcnews.go.com/US/teacher-charged-cyberstalking-students/story?id=13923107

Kris, D. F. (2018, December 2). How to build a trauma-sensitive classroom where all learners feel safe. *KQED*. Retrieved from www.kqed.org/mindshift/52566/how-to-build-a-trauma-sensitive-classroom-where-all-learners-feel-safe

Kusmer, K. (2018). Teacher who stopped attack says he had to save students. *The Daily Herald*. Retrieved from www.dailyherald.com/article/20180527/news/305279904

Kyriacou, C., & Zuin, A. (2016). Cyberbullying of teachers by students on YouTube: challenging the image of teacher authority in the digital age. *Research Papers in Education*, *31*(3), 255–273. http://doi.org/10.1080/02671522.2015.1037337

Lacoe, J., & Steinberg, M. P. (2019). Do suspensions affect student outcomes? *Educational Evaluation and Policy Analysis*, *41*(1), 34–62. https://doi.org/10.3102/0162373718794897

Lieberman, J. (2008). *School shootings: What every parent and educator needs to know to protect our children.* New York, NY: Kensington Publishing Corporation.

Martinson, R. (2020, July 18). Please don't make me risk getting covid-19 to teach your child. *The New York Times.* Retrieved from www.nytimes.com/2020/07/18/opinion/sunday/covid-schools-reopen-teacher-safety.html

McEvoy, A. (2014). Abuse of power. *Teaching Tolerance.* Issue 48, Fall 2014. Retrieved from www.tolerance.org/magazine/fall-2014/abuse-of-power

Miller, C. (2020). *How trauma affects kids in school.* The American Psychological Association. Retrieved from https://childmind.org/article/how-trauma-affects-kids-school/

Mulvahill, E. (2019, September 26). When teachers bully one another. *We Are Teachers.* Retrieved from www.weareteachers.com/teacher-teacher-bullying/

Noddings, N. (2005). *The challenge to care in schools: An alternative approach to education.* New York City: Teachers College Press.

Oltman, G. (2012). *Violence in student writing: A school administrator's guide.* Thousand Oaks: Corwin.

O'Toole, M. E. (1999). The school shooter: A threat assessment perspective. *Federal Bureau of Investigation.* Retrieved from www.fbi.gov/file-repository/stats-services-publications-school-shooter-school-shooter

Pack, L. (2016, March 4). Fighting the anti-snitch culture in schools. *Dayton Daily News.* Retrieved from www.daytondailynews.com/news/crime--law/fighting-the-anti-snitch-culture-schools/Z4b6lBrYCZW2VRW4ql2d2K/

Pandolpho, B. (2020, March 10). Student voice: Simple ways to promote student voice in the classroom. *Edutopia.* Retrieved from www.edutopia.org/article/simple-ways-promote-student-voice-classroom

Parmenter, J. (2018, May 3). *Never fear, teachers! NC Professional Teaching Standards support your presence in Raleigh on May 16.* Notes from the Chalkboard. Retrieved from http://notesfromthechalkboard.com/2018/05/03/never-fear-teachers-nc-professional-teaching-standards-encourage-you-to-be-in-raleigh-on-may-16/

Perry, A. (2018, July 10). When students are better role models than school leaders. *The Hechinger Report*. Retrieved from https://hechingerreport.org/when-students-are-better-role-models-than-school-leaders/utm_source=feedburner&utm_medium=feed&utm_campaign=Feed%3A+HechingerReport+%28Hechinger+Report%29

Rizvi, A. (2019, March 23). American teachers demand voice in school shootings debate. *The National*. Retrieved from www.thenationalnews.com/uae/education/american-teachers-demand-voice-in-school-shootings-debate-1.840577

Rose, J. (2018). Parkland shooting suspect: A story of red flags, ignored. *National Public Radio*. Retrieved from www.npr.org/2018/02/28/589502906/a-clearer-picture-of-parkland-shooting-suspect-comes-into-focus

Rosenberg, E., & Ortenzi, T. (2018, May 27). "Hero" teacher released from hospital after Indiana school shooting, says congresswoman. *The Washington Post*. Retrieved from www.washingtonpost.com/news/post-nation/wp/2018/05/25/students-teacher-swatted-guns-away-tackled-accused-school-shooter-while-suffering-3-gunshot-wounds/

Rothstein-Fisch, C., & Trumbull, E. (2008). *Managing diverse classrooms: How to build on students' cultural strengths*. Alexandria, VA: ASCD.

Roy, L. (2009). *No right to remain silent: What we've learned from the tragedy at Virginia Tech*. New York: Crown Press.

Ruderman, W., & Graham, K. (2019, November 21). Cancer in the classroom. *The Philadelphia Inquirer*. Retrieved from www.inquirer.com/education/a/mesothelioma-philadelphia-school-district-leadirusso-cancer-20191121.html

Sacks, V., & Murphey, D. (2018, February 12). The prevalence of adverse childhood experiences, nationally, by state, and by race or ethnicity. *Child Trends*. Retrieved from www.childtrends.org/publications/prevalence-adverse-childhood-experiences-nationally-state-race-ethnicity

Sexual abuse by teachers is on the rise. (2017, July 11). *The children's center for psychiatry, psychology, & related services*. Retrieved from https://childrenstreatmentcenter.com/sexual-abuse-teachers/

Simpson, M. (2006, September). Teach but don't touch: Practical advice for school employees on avoiding false allegations of improper conduct with students. *NEAToday*. Retrieved from https://nea-nm.org/wp-content/uploads/2018/05/TeachDontTouchColor.pdf

Starratt, R. J. (2004). *Ethical leadership*. San Francisco: Jossey-Bass.

Statista Research Department. (2022, January 4). Number of K-12 school shootings in the United States from 1970 to December 2021, by active shooter status. *Statista Research Services*. Retrieved from www.statista.com/statistics/971473/number-k-12-school-shootings-us/#:~:text=Published%20by%20Statista%20Research%20Department%2C%20Jan%204%2C%202022,the%20highest%20number%20of%20school%20shootings%20since%201970.

Strauss, V. (2015, April 1). How and why convicted Atlanta teachers cheated on standardized tests. *The Washington Post*. Retrieved from www.washingtonpost.com/news/answer-sheet/wp/2015/04/01/how-and-why-convicted-atlanta-teachers-cheated-on-standardized-tests/

Substance Abuse and Mental Health Services Administration. (2022, January 11). *Understanding Child Trauma*. Retrieved from: www.samhsa.gov/child-trauma/understanding-child-trauma

Teacher refuses to lend student a pen during exam, so he plans brutal revenge that gets his teacher fired. (2018, July 5). Bored Panda. Retrieved from www.boredpanda.com/revenge-story-fired-teacher/?utm_source=google&utm_medium=organic&utm_campaign=organic

Thomas, J. R. (2016, December 7). Troubled schools on trial: When poverty permeates the classroom. *CT Mirror*. Retrieved from https://ctmirror.org/2016/12/07/troubled-schools-on-trial-when-poverty-permeates-the-classroom/

Treatment and Services Adaptation Center. (2022). *What is a Trauma Informed School?* Retrieved April 1, 2022, from https://traumaawareschools.org/traumaInSchools

Truong, D. (2019, May 25). 'Borderline criminal': Many public schools teeter on the edge of decrepitude. *The Washington Post*. Retrieved from www.washingtonpost.com/local/eduation/borderline-criminal-thats-the-condition-of-decrepit-public-schools/2019/05/25/bad60064-556f-11e9-814f-e2f46684196e_story.html

Utter, J. (2020, July 28). *Former Moses Lake teacher charged with cyberstalking for allegedly circulating video of student's sexual act*. Retrieved from www.ifiberone.com/columbia_basin/former-moses-lake-teacher-charged-with-cyberstalking-for-allegedly-circulating-video-of-students-sexual-act/article_a528c27c-d12b-11ea-b697-eb45689d90ad.html

Vonow, B. (2015, October 3). Students are using social media to ruin the reputation of schools and staff with defamatory statements. *The Courier Mail*. Retrieved from www.couriermail.com.au/news/students-are-using-social-media-to-ruin-the-reputation-of-schools-and-staff-with-defamatory-statements/news-story/72b0abb6300240fc3dff57d91b0a3902

Whole Child Approach. (2022). The ASCD whole child approach to education whole child. *ASCD*. Retrieved from https://www.ascd.org/whole-child

Willert, T. (2017, November 8). Teacher retention is low at many Oklahoma City district schools. *The Oklahoman*. Retrieved from www.oklahoman.com/story/news/local/oklahoma-city/2017/11/08/teacher-retention-is-low-at-many-oklahoma-city-district-schools/60563349007/

Zakrzewski, V. (2012, September 18). Four ways teachers can show they care. *Greater Good Science Center*. Retrieved from https://greatergood.berkeley.edu/article/item/caring_teacher_student_relationship

Zarra, E. J. (2016). Addressing appropriate and inappropriate teacher-student relationships: A Secondary Education Professional Development Model. *CLEARVoz Journal*, 3(2), 15–29.